W9-BRD-298

# Daily Thoughts for Success

*By*
*Donny Ingram*

*IMG*
*Positive Print Media*

*Daily Thoughts for Success*

Copyright 2012 Ingram Management Group

**Positive Print Media**
96 Hwy 42
Oneonta, AL 35121
**www.ingrammanagement.com/positiveprintmedia**

**Ordering information**
To order additional copies, visit the publisher website. Discounts are available.

**ISBN: 978-0-578-15125-0**

Cover design by: Matt Owens, Threefolddesign.com
Editing & Proofing by: Amber Ingram

**Printed in the United States of America**

# CONTENTS

# COMMENTS

*"Thank you so much for sending these each day. I have been saving your messages and using them to send out to my entire platform and teller associates. Several associates have emailed me back how much they enjoy them. I also have managers using them! So your messages are being spread!"*

Debbie S. Nail
Vice President
Grenada, MS

*"Donny, thanks for your "Thought for the Day" which I not only personally benefit from each and every day, but I forward to my Leadership Team which consist of Branch Managers, Branch Team Leaders, and Branch Service Leaders."*

Mary Doise
Senior Vice President
Houma, LA

*"I send Donny's quotes out to my staff each day to get them started. It's food for the mind. By getting yourself in the right place with the right attitude, your day just goes better. My staff and I look forward to these daily messages."*

DeeAnn Courrege
Consumer Sales Manager
Baton Rouge, LA

*"I just wanted to say thank you for the "Thoughts for the Day". I know that it takes time and commitment to do something like this and you should know that it is very much enjoyed and at the same time extremely beneficial. I find myself looking forward to them as well as sharing them with my group"*

Bea Worden
Senior Vice President
Little Rock, AR

# INTRODUCTION

Over the years I have had many people approach me with the question of how do I stay so motivated all the time? I have even heard them comment that I must have been born motivated. Some people may think that is true but let me tell you it is not. Motivation doesn't just happen. I am a prime example that motivation is a learned behavior. I am naturally an introvert. I would rather spend time alone or with one or two individuals than large groups. It is easy to become enthusiastic especially if you are in the company of a highly motivated individual, but that enthusiasm will quickly disappear if the right principles are not practiced on a continual basis. This takes discipline until it becomes a habit.

I have found that my life will go in the direction of my most predominant thoughts. Therefore, I must continually feed my conscious mind positive thoughts and images. My brain then feeds my subconscious which is connected to my will and emotions. Keeping it filled with the right information is vital to building a positive attitude, thinking more creatively and achieving radical success. I accepted the fact long ago that I could change and when I committed to a pattern of principles and lived by them continually, the change I wanted became permanent.

I hope this book of quotes and thoughts will help inspire and motivate you to keep improving and reaching higher. Your lifestyle will influence others; I hope it is because they want to catch what you have.

# January 1

*"Knowing is not enough, we must apply.*
*Willing is not enough, we must do."*
Johann Wolfgang von Goethe

Can you think of a time that you watched something happen without standing up for what you truly believe? It is not enough to just know what you believe in. You must be willing to use your passion to fuel your success. Even if it is doing some small simple action, you must DO it. Think about what you really believe in and then make a stance for that belief. Even if you just choose someone else to share your beliefs with, it is a start!

# January 2

*"The only way to lead people is to show them a vision of*
*where you're headed and a path to get there together.*
*These days people don't commit to companies*
*or colleges, they commit to other people.*
*That's the name of the game."*
Dr. Howard Tullman

Great leadership is vital to an organizations growth and success. When people buy into the leader's vision they commit to see it through to completion. When leaders can effectively draw a picture of the end result and how it will benefit everyone, then people have purpose and from purpose will come passion and passion is the fuel for success.

## January 3

*"Twenty years from now you will be more disappointed by the things you didn't do than by the ones you did do. So throw off the bowlines. Sail away from the safe harbor. Catch the trade winds in your sails.*
*Explore! Dream! Discover!"*
Mark Twain

What would you do if you knew you could not fail? What is stopping you? As we get older, many of us appreciate the things we have had the opportunity to do…but we also tend to regret the things we didn't do. Don't let this happen to you. Build your vision and allow yourself to do the things you really want to do.

## January 4

*"You get credit for what you finish,*
*not what you start."*
Unknown

Some say the hardest part is getting started. If this is true, why do we hear stories of people who give up on their diet, stop writing a novel or quit a difficult task at work? Maybe it's not the start but the finish that's so difficult. This is important to know when you are chasing after a dream or goal. Remind yourself that if it were easy, everyone would do it. So keep at your goals, and be prepared for the bumps along the way.

## January 5

*"People are always blaming their circumstances for where and what they are. The people who really make it in this world are the ones who get up and look for the circumstances they want and if they can't find them, they make a choice to take a chance to bring about the change they want."*
Donny Ingram

Is there a situation you wish you weren't in? Change it. Look for the positives and realize that life presents many lessons to learn. Make the choice; take the chance to do things that will bring about the change you desire. Go for what you really want out of life. Magic can happen.

## January 6

*"There's a difference between interest and commitment. When you're interested in doing something, you do it only when it's convenient. When you're committed to something, you accept no excuses; only results."*
Kenneth Blanchard

Are you interested in your goals, or are you fully committed? One of the most common complaints among goal setters nowadays is that there's just not enough time. Don't wait for a vague time in the future when other things won't get in the way or when it's more convenient. If your goals are important don't let anything stand in your way.

## January 7

***"Vision without action is just a day dream, but action
without vision is a nightmare."***
Unknown

We must have a vision of where we are going and what
exactly it is we want to achieve. With that we can set out
to plan, prepare and expect to reach our destiny. I believe
the 6-P formula is important to remember and follow in our
journey – "Proper    Prior    Planning    Prevents    Poor
Performance." Planning to succeed is vital to reach our
goals in life. Get a vision, write down your goals and put a
plan together and then take ACTION, take "MASSIVE
ACTION."

## January 8

***"Everything depends upon execution;
having just a vision is not a solution"***
Stephen Sondheim

We seem to talk a lot about setting goals and developing a
plan which are extremely important steps in achieving
success. But we forget sometimes to stress the execution
strategy. Without putting action behind our goals and plans
there will be no result and results is what we should be
looking for and expecting. In all our efforts let us plan,
prepare, develop and execute our success strategy.

4

## January 9

*"The way you think, the way you behave, the way you eat, can influence your life by 30 -50 years."*
Deepak Chopra

It would be great if we all took this to heart as a teenager. First of all, thinking properly is a vital key to becoming successful. As a human we can only hold one thought at a time so we should make each thought count. Physiologists tell us that our life will go in the direction of our most predominant thoughts, so meditate on the positive not the negative. Think right thoughts and eat healthier so you can live life to its fullest, live longer, be more productive and be the example for others to follow.

## January 10

*"The average human being in any line of work could double his productive capacity overnight if he began right now to do all the things he knows he should do, and to stop doing all the things he knows he should not do."*
Elmer G. Letterman

How can you apply this piece of wisdom to your everyday routine? As John Maxwell recommends, you need to "Audit" yourself and reinvent your daily routine. Talented people are always striving to do a little more. Therefore, focus your efforts, manage your time, define your talents, and be flexible enough to change the things that need changing. Create that little extra that can take you from just being ordinary to becoming an extraordinary performer.

## January 11

### *"If you rest, you rust."*
Helen Hayes

As a leader, speaker or manager, don't assume your communication skills are good enough. Miscommunication is too detrimental to any organization, any career and especially to your personal relationships. Always practice good communication. Mastering communication is vital and you have the power to do so.

---

## January 12

### *"It is not the length of life, but the depth of life."*
Ralph Waldo Emerson

Do you think that it takes years and years to accomplish great things? Maybe in certain instances this is true, but magical things can happen each and every day. What are you doing to make your life worthwhile? Are you doing anything to benefit others, or just focusing on yourself? We can't be guaranteed that tomorrow will come, but we can be guaranteed that if we work hard, we can make a difference in the lives of others. This should be important to each of us while we have the chance, while we have the means and the energy? Then let's do it. Don't wait. Do it every day of your life.

## January 13

### *"Little words never hurt a big idea."*
Howard Newton

It takes a large collection of small goals to add up to a big goal. We all need to follow through with these smaller goals to achieve our main objectives. However, don't think your big goals are in jeopardy if you don't achieve all of your smaller goals. Obviously, we want to accomplish all of our small goals if possible, but it's also important to keep these goals in prospective. The ultimate mission is the long-term goal, so remember to keep this in mind and not to get discouraged when you miss a couple of smaller ones.

## January 14

### *"Never be bullied into silence. Never allow yourself to be made a victim. Accept no one's definition of your life; define yourself."*
Harvey Fierstein

Have you ever let the opinions of others determine your path in life? It is easy to be consumed by social pressure and to leave your life on a back burner. It's important to define what you want to do with your life and you should do it based on how your creator made you. We should be defined by our design and the purpose for which our abilities are needed. Do not accept it when others tell you which path you should take. Define yourself!

## January 15

*"Be a lifelong student. The more you learn, the more you earn and the more self-confidence you will have."*
Brian Tracy

We should never stop learning. No one will ever really "arrive" as some think they will. If we expect to be fulfilled and have influence and success then we should always be like a sponge and soak up as much knowledge and experience as possible. Contrary to popular belief old dogs can learn new tricks. Being an "Old dog" myself, I don't ever want to stop learning. Then and only then will we be prepared to do more, be more and ultimately have more in this life.

## January 16

*"Energy & persistence conquer all things."*
Benjamin Franklin

Consistency is an action that is often overlooked by society. You probably don't hear people telling you to be consistent in order to accomplish your goals. This quote reminds us that persistence and energy can conquer anything. Some days you may not feel like doing anything, stay consistent and push ahead anyway. Set a streak for yourself and see how long you can go completing your goals. Consistency with energy is a powerful tool for completing any task, especially your goals...so use it whenever you get a chance.

## January 17

*"Do not be afraid to ask dumb questions.*
*They are easier to handle than dumb mistakes."*
Unknown

Asking a silly question in front of a large group and getting laughed at is a fear we all have. We feel like everyone will look down on us and think we're stupid, so we hold our tongue and possibly mess something up later. Then we question why we didn't speak up in the first place. Questions are a part of learning so feel free to speak up. You can still learn without asking questions, but it's called the hard way for a reason.

## January 18

*"Good advice for anyone wanting to make an impact*
*with a product, a service or even a message is to*
*differentiate yourself."*
Donny Ingram

Think for a minute, what is so important about you, your product, and your company? Most business people want to make an impression and be memorable to everyone they meet. Call me crazy, but I don't want to talk to someone who wants to manage my account, develop my business, or engineer my sale. I want to communicate with someone who desires to fulfill my needs or solve my problems. Being different from the competition is the key to success. Whatever way you choose it must differentiate you from others by leaving a positive impression.

## January 19

*"Sometimes it's hard to determine where to draw the line between being nice and not hurting people's feelings, and standing up for what you believe."*
Donny Ingram

Have you ever held back from saying what you truly believe because you thought it might cause hurt feelings or upset someone because you didn't see things as they did? We get in trouble by not standing up for what we believe. In many instances we have allowed the few to set the standard for us all. Take a stand for what you truly believe. Don't be obnoxious and rude but politely speak out, be determined and committed to walk the walk as well as talk the talk.

## January 20

*"If at first you don't succeed, you're running about average."*
Author Unknown

Sure, try, try again. That's great advice. Don't give up, though, because you aren't a failure. Success doesn't' just happen. It can take several tries before you even begin to make some progress. Do you think this doesn't happen to anybody else? It does! We all come across roadblocks in life, whether big, little, short, or long-term. We all find them. Some of us give up, but some keep trudging along. Which will you do? If everything just happened with ease, would anything be worth working for?

10

## January 21

*"Wisdom is knowing what to do next, skill is knowing how to do it, and virtue is doing it."*
Anonymous

Most resolutions set January 1 are history by February 1. But tips and ideas alone won't get it done. It's funny how all the time, energy, and resources seem to be put into setting goals, while their actual achievement is just expected to take care of itself. Without a concrete plan and the right resources, it's too easy to fall back into old habits. Real change takes time – and needs help. Surround yourself with reminders that make your goals tough to ignore and impossible to forget. You're accountable to yourself and nobody else. After all, goal achievement is something you do year-round, not just in January.

## January 22

*"Only those who dare to fail greatly can ever achieve greatly."*
Robert F. Kennedy

Do you take any risks in your life? Do you set your goals high, and then work hard to reach them? If not, how much progress can you be making? Of course, there is always a slight chance that you might fail, but you will have learned invaluable lessons along the way. So don't be scared to have high expectations for yourself. If you have reached one goal, set another one. Smaller victories along your path will lead to greater ones.

## January 23

*"Everybody is like a magnet. You attract to yourself reflections of that which you are. If you're friendly then everybody else seems to be friendly too."*
Dr. David Hawkins

Ever hear the phrase, "Misery loves company"? Well it's true and miserable people will attract other miserable people. The same is true for positive people, motivated people, interesting people, loving people, successful people etc. Take a look at who you are, you're actions and the attitude you exhibit and if that is not the kind of people you wish to attract then make the decision today to change.

## January 24

*"Invest 3% of your income in yourself (self-development) in order to guarantee your future."*
Brian Tracy

Most people do not think about investing a portion of their income into themselves, but in order to grow, excel in your profession and achieve your true potential you must practice self-development. Don't expect your company to provide you all the education, training and motivation you're going to need. Putting 3% of your income into yourself will help assure you of achieving your goals and becoming the person you were designed to become. If you want to be significant, influential and successful then invest in you!

# January 25

## *"One man with courage makes a majority."*
Andrew Jackson

Are you waiting for permission from someone else before you can pursue your goals and dreams? Hoping you'll get the okay to stop what you're doing and start doing what you really love? You don't need to wait. All you need is a vision to follow, a plan of action and the brave decision to get started. It takes courage to follow a dream, and you have to give yourself permission first. You have more at stake in your own life than anyone else does. Keep in mind, you can plan, prepare and expect success right where you are today.

# January 26

## *"Fortune favors the bold"*
Juvenal

Good things happen to good people, right? Sometimes this is true. However, it could also be said that good things happen to those that work for them. You are not simply a passive player in the game of life, but have the ability to serve an active role. Sometimes you have to go out and search for what you want out of life. Things will not always just happen on their own. Hoping for a promotion for example? You have to show your boss exactly what you are made of. Exert yourself and you'll get a lot of what you desire.

## January 27

### *"We're always getting ready to live, but never living."*
Anonymous

There is no lesson for today. You have permission to stop thinking for a moment and just enjoy yourself. Stop and go look at the world. Rediscover the natural wonders that you walk past every day. Let your mind be grateful for a break. Don't think, don't strain. Let the memories of loved ones remind you of your favorite times. Close your eyes and listen to your heart beat in your ears. See the hope, the alarm, the love, the grief in faces that stream by. Thank your creator for the chance to even be here. For a moment today, don't worry about being greater or better or slimmer, just be!

## January 28

### *"Here's the test to find whether your mission on Earth is finished: if you're alive, it isn't."*
Richard Back

That's the great thing about being involved in something that's bigger and more important than yourself – you'll never run out of meaningful things to do! The unimportant stuff can be checked off or forgotten about once it's done. A personal mission or purpose is so key to your being that it's impossible to forget or put down for very long. What that purpose is can be different for each of us, and can change over time. Your mission is already inside you. What would bring the most meaning to your life? Go do it!

# January 29

*"If you don't see yourself as a winner, then you cannot perform as a winner."*
Zig Ziglar

You cannot expect others to believe that you are skilled, talented, beautiful, sexy and successful until you believe it. Dr. Joyce Brothers says, "You cannot consistently perform in a manner than is inconsistent with the way you see yourself." See yourself for who you really are. You are "Fearfully and wonderfully made" so see what your creator sees – perfection and greatness!

# January 30

*"When we are motivated by goals that have deep meaning, by dreams that need completion, by pure love that needs expressing, then we truly live life."*
Greg Anderson

What motivates you to live life? Are you motivated by deadlines and things that you HAVE to do or by dreams and things that you want to do? If you find yourself losing site of your goals and dreams, take a minute to ask yourself why you are letting things get in your way. Set aside some time to think about your goals. What do you dream of doing? Set goals to help you get there. When you are working toward a goal or dream that has significance to you, you will have more passion to fuel your fire allowing you to create daily successes for yourself!

# January 31

***"There are two kinds of man: the ones who make history and the ones who endure it"***
Camilo Jose Cela

History is written all around you every day. It may not be history that makes the college textbooks, but it's your history just the same. Do you make your own history? Or do you endure the life that others make for you? When you decide to have a good day, you create a life you want. There are so many different possible histories out there just waiting to be lived. Whatever your life has been up to this point doesn't matter. What counts is the history that awaits you in the future. Which do you choose?

# February 1

***"There are only two options regarding commitment. You're either IN or you're OUT. There's no such thing as life in-between."***
Pat Riley

Your life deserves better than a half-hearted effort. Since you probably don't want to look back on a life full of "almost made it" memories, you must have total commitment. There is nothing more satisfying than giving everything you've got, reaching your total limit, and then realizing that you really did it. Your first goal should be to build a life that you can get "INTO". Then don't look back. Make every day count and live with purpose, energy, and live it completely.

## February 2

*"Work like you don't need the money.  Love like you've never been hurt.  Dance like nobody's watching."*
Satchel Paige

Take a minute and think about this quote. Are you able to follow these three life instructions? Do you live to work, or work to live?  This week, adapt a new attitude, work like you don't need the money. You might find yourself able to be more efficient and have more fun at the office. This week try to love like you've never been hurt. Have you ever been at home listening to your favorite CD and started dancing? Use that same energy this week to be yourself wherever you go!

## February 3

*"In the field of observation, chance favors only the prepared mind"*
Louis Pasteur

When life gives you options and opens doors, will you be up to the challenge? You could be the luckiest stiff in the world.  Your fingers could have the golden touch; you might always have the wind at your back and the sun never in your eyes. But if you don't recognize opportunities for what they are, or you're not prepared, it won't matter a lick. Life's opportunities demand action. It's a matter of being prepared. You can get yourself ready by building a strong body and mind, creating confidence and developing some healthy habits.  So….are you ready?

## February 4

*"What a man accomplishes in a day depends upon the way in which he approaches his tasks."*
Arland Gilbert

Do you go to work each day grudgingly, or do you approach things with a cheerful attitude and view them as challenges? This distinction can really make a difference. You'll waste more energy complaining about or dreading something than if you were to just go ahead and get it done. Be a doer, put your head in it and watch what you can accomplish. The time will pass quickly. So have the right attitude. Whistle while you work.

## February 5

*"Snowflakes are one of nature's most fragile things, but just look what they can do when they stick together."*
Vista M. Kelly

A single individual is capable of amazing things in this world, like severing their own arm that is trapped under a boulder to stay alive, or inventing electricity. But when a group of individuals come together to form a working unit, this can turn into magic. Interaction amongst others can develop new ideas spurred off other ones. Construction becomes easier; long projects become shorter, the possibilities are endless. A good team or group does not work well together automatically; they have to work at working well together. Remember the power of one is great, but the power of many is even greater.

## February 6

### *"The man who wants to lead the orchestra must turn his back on the crowd."*
James Crook

Everybody wants the fame and attention for a job well done. As almost everyone has come to find out though, fame and attention does not come all the time. For every great player making it onto Sports Center for every game-winning shot, there are a million Joe Smiths out there, doing wonderful things to lead others but receiving no credit. If you are finding yourself upset by the lack of attention you're getting for your leadership, perhaps it's time to reevaluate why you are a leader in the first place. True leaders lead to help their team, their community, their office; not for fame and attention. Those watching will soon forget what you have done, but those you are leading will remember what you've done for them long after you are gone.

## February 7

### *"Coming together is a beginning; keeping together is progress; working together is success."*
Anonymous

Take a minute and think about all of the great things that have been accomplished with a team. Having a partner to share your goals, celebrate your victories, and to work through problems can help you reach your dreams! Sometimes we forget that this process is more than just coming together. Coming together is the first step to a successful relationship. You must work to keep it together and find new ways to work together to complete tasks.

## February 8

*"A ship in the harbor is safe.*
*But that's not what ships are built for."*
Anonymous

We all want to stick with our normal, commonplace routines because we feel secure. By doing so we may miss out on new opportunities. In 1975, a third-year student at Harvard University decided to drop out and pursue something else. The student's name was Bill Gates. He saw an opportunity and acted upon it. While this does not mean every time you explore something new you will become a billionaire, it shows that some of the world's geniuses even took a chance on their dreams. If you are waiting around for your goals or your dream to just fall into your lap, it could take awhile. So, break from the norm and cast your ship down uncharted waters.

## February 9

*"Behold the turtle. He only makes progress*
*when he sticks his neck out.*
James Bryant Conant

If it's been said before, it's been said 937 times – if you want to succeed, you are going to have to take chances. The turtle for example moves as fast as a rock. He has a choice; he could stay inside his shell all day and relax and miss out on the action or stick his head out and do something about it. When we stay complacent with our lives, we are the ones relaxing inside the shell. We are missing out on the action. However, if you stick your neck out of the shell, there are so many possibilities waiting for you.

20

# February 10

### *"Hire great people and give them the freedom to be awesome."*
Andrew Mason

Far too often we hire great people then we stifle their commitment and creativity due to company policy, guidelines or something much worse like jealousy, self-esteem or fear. People want to be appreciated for their ideas even if their ideas are not put into practice. They want to feel part of the organization and believe they are valued for what they know and can do. As a leader/manager of people it's your responsibility to relate to them how valuable they are to the organization. They will never forget you for it!

# February 11

### *"There are only two ways to live your life. One is as though nothing is a miracle. The other is as if everything is."*
Albert Einstein

Do you appreciate or ignore the miracles around you every day? For some reason, it's hard to be impressed with anything these days. When nothing is "special", boredom and gloom aren't far behind. Look around where you're sitting right now, and try to see it for the first time. Think about the human potential that created the stuff in the room. Think about the miracles of nature right outside your window. Think about how amazing it is that you're even here to see it.

## February 12

### *"Three things in life that, once gone, never come back - Time, Words & Opportunity"*
Author Unknown

If time is money then how are you spending it? Make every moment of every day count. Words are powerful and they can give life or death to ideas, emotions, and actions. Don't miss opportunities that come your way. They may be in the form of someone needing help, a business transaction, or just an encouraging word to lift up a friend. Don't let these be wasted today.

## February 13

### *"Yes, risk taking is inherently failure-prone. Otherwise, it would be called sure-thing-taking."*
Tim McMahon

What are the odds of winning the lottery? More than a million to one, right? Yet every week so many people willingly buy tickets because of the tiny chance at winning it big. "What's the worst that could happen?" They don't win! I'm not a lottery player but my point is the attitude of those that do. If you pursue a goal and fail, are you any worse off than before? No! But, if we only settled for sure things, how empty would our lives be? Remember, the only time you are guaranteed to fail is when you do not even make the attempt. So take that chance, it could end up being the success story you talk about for the next 10 years.

## February 14

*"Courage is not the absence of fear, but rather the judgment that something else is more important than fear.*
Ambrose Redmoon

We are all scared of something. There is no denying that. Fear is a natural emotion. Maybe it is something small and seemingly silly, like an apprehension of spiders. Sometimes fear can be so large it can almost paralyze you. How do you react to it? If you see something wrong going on around you, fear can sometimes stop you from taking action to stop it. What will you do? Courage and bravery dictate that you stand up for what you know is right, even if doing so causes you anxiety. Be firm with what you believe. Sometimes you have to help those that cannot help themselves.

## February 15

*"Mistakes are the portals of discovery."*
James Joyce

Most of us have heard the saying "learn by your mistakes," but how many of us actually do? Making a mistake is one of the best opportunities you have to learn about your task and about yourself. When being interviewed Andrew Carnegie was asked, "What has made you so successful?" He responded, "Mistakes, I try to never make the same one twice." The next time you make a mistake take a minute to think about it. What can I do to make sure this doesn't happen again? What did I learn from this mistake? Never let fear stop you!

## February 16

*"Ability is what you are capable of doing.*
*Motivation determines what you do.*
*Attitude determines how well you do it."*
Lou Holtz

While we can build and improve our abilities we must keep our eyes on the goal in order to stay motivated. But a positive attitude is the one element that can assure us of either achieving what we want or failing miserably. Get up every morning and look yourself in the mirror and say, "God look how great you made me, I'm going to do more today than I have ever done before." A positive attitude will be a magnet in attracting the right people who can and will assist you in accomplishing whatever you desire.

## February 17

*"Most all successful people are big dreamers. They imagine what their future could be and then they work with passion and purpose toward that vision."*
Donny Ingram

All my life I've encountered people who didn't believe in dreaming big. It does take more than dreaming to be successful, but without a dream there is no goal, no motivation and no plan. I saw a sign once that read, "Vision without action is just a daydream, but action without vision is a nightmare." How true! Dreaming big is great but you must put legs to your dreams, put a plan together and start moving toward the goal.

## February 18

*"People often say that motivation doesn't last. Well, neither does bathing – that's why we recommend it daily."*
Zig Ziglar

Makes sense doesn't it? The secret to staying consistent with your goals is to stay motivated. That means finding ways to fire yourself up on a daily basis. Give yourself those little positive reminders that you have a job to do and a good reason for doing it. What's pushing you? Is it a specific milestone, your self-esteem, a drive to make a difference? Surround yourself with visual, verbal and physical "pep talks" that trigger that motive. A daily dose of motivation kicks off the dust before it can settle and gives you a fresh, clean start.

---

## February 19

*"Life is not easy for any of us, but what of that? We must have perseverance and, above all, confidence in ourselves."*
Marie Curie

We all come across obstacles, some anticipated and some unexpected. Perhaps once in a while an obstacle will disappear on its own, but don't count on it. Usually, it's going to come down to you to make it happen. With hard work and the right attitude, you have everything you need to overcome and win. Try and look forward to the next time a roadblock comes your way; instead of an obstacle, think of it as a challenge. Then get after it!

## February 20

### *"You are the only person on earth who can use your ability."*
Zig Ziglar

We are all born with certain qualities and characteristics that enable us to perform and fulfill our intended purpose. No one else can use what you are designed with. Think about a product being developed, the builder normally uses the products intended purpose to govern the design, function and nature of that product. We humans are no different; our creator built into us the gifts, talents, skills and abilities to perform in a specific way. Therefore, realize you are specifically designed to use your abilities in becoming successful in your purpose.

## February 21

### *"Thoughts produce actions and actions produce results"*
Donny Ingram

As a human you can only hold one thought at a time. Therefore you need to make every thought count. The Bible even tells us to think on things that are good, holy, pure and positive. You should not allow negative, demoralizing and unethical thoughts to remain in your brain. When you do they cause an overwhelming negative feeling that will not aid you in moving in the direction you need to be moving. On the other hand by thinking right thoughts it will have a positive effect and the results you want will follow.

## February 22

### *"Passion produces profits"*
Donny Ingram

As a leader you must be passionate in order for the rest of the organization to be passionate. When you exhibit passion then your followers will get involved in fanning the flames. They will begin to really fan the flames of passion when they are empowered to get involved in developing a strategy and knowing their work impacts the organization as a whole and their involvement in making a difference in the community. Employees are the frontline to the business, the community and customers, so their passion is what bleeds through and it is their passion that brings the results you want and need in today's tough marketplace.

---

## February 23

### *"Remember you will not always win. Some days, the most resourceful individuals will taste defeat. But there is, in this case, always tomorrow - after you have done your best to achieve success today."*
Maxwell Maltz

Very seldom, if ever, will you find anyone who never fails, never loses a game, or a sale. However, I have found that people who are successful never let defeat hinder their momentum and focus. This takes discipline, good self-communication and most of all setting a standard of excellence. Live and work with excellence and experience success!

## February 24

*"It doesn't matter where you are coming from.*
*All that matters is where you are going."*
Brian Tracy

Never allow your past to hinder your future. For some it may be social status, for others it may be the lack of education or finances, for a few it may be their appearance, for whatever reason you must let it go. The past is history focus on the present and the future. People like Mahatma Gandhi, Mother Teresa, Albert Schweitzer, Martin Luther King Jr., Daniel "Chappie" James and hundreds of others didn't let their past stop them from achieving greatness and leaving their mark on the world. Neither should you.

## February 25

*"Just keep going. Everybody gets better*
*if they keep at it."*
Ted Williams

Perseverance and persistence is the key to becoming excellent at your craft and success is a by-product of excellence. The old saying, "quitters never win and winners never quit" is correct. To achieve what you really want in life you must never give up. It's like asking a young mother when she is going to give up on her baby walking, she'll tell you with no hesitation - NEVER. That is the confidence we must have to achieve success; never quit until you achieve your goal. You may have to change your approach several times but never quit.

## February 26

*"The champion wins first, then walks into the arena.*
*Everybody else walks into the arena and then tries to*
*figure out what to do"*
Jim Fannin

Becoming successful and being a consistent winner requires discipline in thinking. You must see it in your mind before it will ever become a reality in the natural. Your life will go in the direction of your most predominate thoughts so disciplining yourself to think correctly is a major factor to achieving the things you really want out of life. Start today to imagine everything happening as you want them and expect to achieve the results you desire.

## February 27

*"If you want to achieve anything you must first see the*
*result in your own mind before it will become a reality."*
Donny Ingram

It has been proven over and over that as a human we achieve things much easier when visualizing the result before taking action. I know for me this is very true. When I see what I want and begin to meditate on it and visualize it happening it seems much more likely that I'll get the desired outcome. As Tony Robbins has said many times, "80% of building wealth is physiological and 20% mechanics." How we think is so important to how we live and how successful we become in achieving our dreams. Start today to visualize the results you want in every situation.

## February 28

***"Don't limit yourself. Many people limit themselves to what they think they can do. You can go as far as your mind lets you. What you believe, remember, you can achieve."***
Mary Kay Ash

Have you ever had a dream of doing something and thinking to yourself, "I can't do that" or "I'd love to but…" We all have real limitations especially in the physical realm, but so many people allow things like education, finances, family or friends, limit what they are capable of doing and doing well. I have found that People who succeed know ***what*** they want; ***why*** they want it and they form a ***plan*** and put that plan into action. Most of all they ***measure*** their progress. If they're not moving toward their goal they simply change their approach. They keep changing until they get what they want.

## March 1

***"In today's world, nobody achieves success alone. It takes teamwork to succeed."***
Donny Ingram

One of the major factors that will determine how successful we become are the people we meet. No one can do it by themselves. People are influential and can accelerate or hinder your career. They can open doors and provide opportunities that are otherwise impossible. People are important because every dollar we earn will come from someone else. Therefore, honing your people skills should be a priority.

## March 2

*"Friendship is like a BOOK.  It takes few seconds to burn,*
*but it takes years to write."*
Author Unknown

The old saying "To have a friend you must be a friend" is truly accurate.  Friends are very important in our lives, we need them because as a human we need to be connected to others and having friends fills that need.  A best friend however can be truly important.  For me it is my spouse.  I know there are many who cannot say that, but some of us have been able to cultivate a phenomenal friendship with the one closest to us.    Having your spouse as your best friend is one of the greatest gifts in life.

## March 3

*"In the chase between a lion and a deer....*
*Many times the deer wins.... Because the lion runs for*
*food but the deer runs for life.*
*Remember; "Purpose is more important than need"...*
Anonymous

Purpose is the driving force behind everything we do.  It is the reason we work at a certain job or pursue a certain career.  The hobbies we enjoy, the relationships we form as well as the power to persevere come from our purpose in life.  Purpose gives us confidence to keep on keeping on.  Purpose will provide contentment in our pursuit and assist us in refusing to turn away for something that might appear easier.  And lastly, purpose will bring passion, and passion is the fuel needed for success.

31

## March 4

### *"Success is not what you think it is…*
### *It is what you believe it is"*
Doug Firebaugh

What we believe will determine our actions and our actions will determine where we go in every area of our lives. The old saying, "Put the right stuff in and get the right stuff out" is correct. We must focus on the right information which will form our beliefs that strengthen our motivation to continue. Don't listen to negative and demoralizing conversations from people who have never done what you are attempting. Read about and listen to people who have done it, people who are doing it and keep focused on the positive. There is little we cannot accomplish when we believe we can.

## March 5

### *"We are what we repeatedly do.*
### *Excellence, therefore, is not an act, but a habit."*
Aristotle

As a human we form habits over time that can be changed, but it takes effort and sometime that effort produces great pain. However, if you want to be successful, talented, skilled and significant then you must set excellence as your standard. That means your thinking must change, which changes your action, which will bring about the desired result. According to the experts it takes about a month to form a habit. Determine what needs to change in your life and start the actions necessary to form the habits that will lead you down the road to excellence.

## March 6

*"Today's world situation requires strong men to stand up and be counted – no matter what their personal grievances are. Our greatest weapon is one we have always possessed – our heritage of freedom, our unity as a nation."*
General Daniel "Chappie" James

General Chappie James was the first African American Four Star General in the United States Air Force. His statement so many years ago still holds true today. We must stand up and let our values, our morals and our beliefs be counted regardless of who it offends. Thousands have fought and died to give us that right to stand and we fail them if we don't use that opportunity to do so. Our children are depending on us to set the stage for them. Will you be the example to follow?

## March 7

*"Time is always in short supply. There is no substitute for time. Everything requires time. It is the only universal condition. All work takes place in, and uses up time. Yet most people take for granted this unique, irreplaceable and necessary resource."*
Peter Drucker

I believe Christine Warren summed it up best when she wrote, *"I have only just a minute, only sixty seconds in it. Forced upon me, can't refuse it. Didn't seek it, didn't choose it. But it's up to me to use it; I must suffer if I lose it, give account if I abuse it. Just a tiny little minute, but eternity is in it."* What will you spend your 86,400 seconds doing this day. Make every moment count!

33

## March 8

***"The common denominator of success – the secret of success of every man who has ever been successful – lies in the fact that he formed the habit of doing things that failures don't like to do."***
Albert E.N. Gray

Nearly two centuries ago, American theologian Nathanael Emmons commented that *"habit is either the best servants or the worst of masters."* Those who would become successful, then, will be wise to choose those servants who will be of the greatest help in reaching their goals.

## March 9

***"Most people do not listen with the intent to understand; they listen with the intent to reply"***
Stephen Covey

To be an effective communicator you must be a good listener. When I think of listening I think of selling. As a sales manager and trainer I like how one expert summed up the value of listening in terms of income earned. His study showed that an <u>average</u> salesperson listened only 20% of the time and talked 80% earning an average of $24,000 per year. A <u>good</u> salesperson listened 50% of the time and talked 50% and earned an average of $54,000 annually. However, an <u>excellent</u> salesperson listened 80% of the time and talked on 20% earning over $100,000 per year. The power of communication is listening!

## March 10

*"If the people let government decide what foods they eat
and what medicines they take, their bodies will soon
be in as sorry a state as are the souls of those who
live under tyranny."*
Thomas Jefferson

With all the information available today we should not be a
nation of unhealthy people. We need to stop taking the
FDA's advice as well as the drug companies on what to put
into our bodies. Slow down on the fast food and eat more
of the good stuff. Get away from Facebook, TV and
Twitter and walk more. Take back what is being taken
from you! NOW!

## March 11

*"The future is not something we enter.
The future is something we create."*
Leonard I. Sweet

So many people are waiting to see what the future holds for
their career, their family and their community. Have you
ever thought about creating your future? If you know
where you want to be next year, in five years or even
twenty years then you can start today to develop and create
what it takes to achieve that result. The problem is most
folks really do not know where they want to be, oh, they
will tell you they do, but they have no real plan in place to
get there. For example, many say they want to go to
heaven but they're life style says something different. Take
control, start today to plan, prepare and take action to have
the future you desire. And most of all expect it to happen!

35

## March 12

*Faith is not trying to believe something regardless of the evidence: Faith is daring to do something regardless of the consequences."*
Sherwood Eddy

So many people talk about having faith. Faith is really an action word. If you truly believe something your actions will dictate moving in that direction. Therefore, believe in yourself, your talents, skills and abilities and take action on what you truly believe and watch the miraculous take place. Studies have proven that if you really believe something it will change the environment around you. I urge you to put your faith to work and experience the exhilaration of victory.

---

## March 13

*"When you make a choice, you change the future."*
Deepak Chopra

John Maxwell says, "We are a sum total of all the choices we've made in our past." Most people never think about how every decision can affect their future. They only worry about how it affects them now. Therefore, you can sometimes make decisions that have long-term consequences and take you down a path you didn't want. It's time to realize that if you don't like where you are you must start to make better quality decisions. Look ahead and try to determine where every decision will take you before committing your life to it.

## March 14

### *"People who fight fire with fire usually end up with ashes"*
Abigail Van Buren

Far too many people want to settle the score and strike back at the people who offend abuse or embarrass them. When we retaliate with the same no one wins, everyone loses. Don't lower yourself to other people's standards. Don't get burned, forgive and forget.

## March 15

### *"Time is more valuable than money. You can get more money, but you cannot get more time"*
Jim Rohn

The most valuable resource in our possession is time. How we use it will determine our success. It is the one thing we can never regain; when it is gone it is gone. We each are given 86,400 seconds each day, what we spend it on is important. Spend it wisely!

## March 16

### *"You might well remember that nothing can bring you success but yourself"*
Napoleon Hill

We are each responsible for achieving our own goals reaching our own destiny and fulfilling our dreams. No one can do it for us; we must answer the call ourselves. Live with PRIDE, Personal Responsibility In Developing Excellence, and you can live a life of health, wealth and joy.

## March 17

### *"You cannot consistently perform in a manner that is inconsistent with the way you see yourself"*
Dr. Joyce Brothers

The image you have of yourself is one of the most important factors in achieving your goals. Do not believe what others may say, build your self-image by telling yourself how great you are and what you will accomplish every day of your life. Get up every morning and look yourself in the mirror and say, "God look how great you made me, today I'll..."

# March 18

*"Invest whatever is necessary to create the atmosphere that motivates you and remind yourself continuously that there is something in those around you that you have not yet discerned."*
Mike Murdock

How you feel and how effective and motivational you are depends a great deal on your surroundings. Therefore, you must create the atmosphere that gives you energy and fosters your creativity. And most of all communicate to yourself how valuable you are as well as those around you.

# March 19

*"Love me or hate me, both are in my favor. If you love me, I'll always be in your heart. If you hate me, I'll always be in your mind.*
Unknown

"Wow" moments are important especially to those you want to remember you. We can all be remembered for something, the key is make it valuable not detestable.

## March 20

**"Today is a gift so before you complain about all the things that is going wrong why not just give God thanks for all the things that are going right."**
Unknown

The attitude of gratitude is one that many say led them to be such a success. I believe it is the most important characteristic we can portray. Being grateful and giving others thanks will open doors and lead to more opportunities than you could ever imagine.

## March 21

**"Always look at what you have left. Never look at what you have lost."**
Robert H. Schuller

In today's modern world we are taught to value things. We are led to believe that the more things we get the happier we'll become. Nothing is farther from the truth. As my beautiful wife told me years ago, "It's not how much you have that makes you wealthy; it's how little you need."

## March 22

*"To give anything less than your best
is to sacrifice the gift."*
Steve Roland Prefontaine

Never give up, never give out, and never give in, only give your best. When you have given your best you have done all you are designed to do and success will be yours.

## March 23

*"Lucky people get opportunities; Brave people create
opportunities; and Winners are those that convert
problems into opportunities."*
Author Unknown

Everyone wants to be a winner. Winners see things differently. Winners develop an attitude that says, "What is great about this, and how can I make it better." That attitude will open your eyes to see opportunities that others cannot.

# March 24

## *"Perception is based on what you believe, but it does not affect the real truth."*
Donny Ingram

If you're not getting the results you desire, then perhaps it's because of what you believe. Keep in mind that your behavior is driven by your beliefs therefore; your life is a reflection of what you believe. The primary reason your life is the way it is, is because of your perception; and the reason for your perception may be because you have not fully seen or understood the actual truth of the matter. The truth is what we should all be seeking then our beliefs will drive our actions and lead us to the proper conclusion and success.

# March 25

## *"Discipline is the bridge between goals and accomplishments."*
Jim Rohn

We have all known people who think that one day they are just going to wake up one morning and "POOF" they have arrived with all the things they desire. That will never happen without some discipline in your life. People who succeed in life and business today have disciplined themselves to do certain things, probably things that are not so comfortable for them. Doing those things is necessary if you really want to achieve your goal. How much discipline do you have? Will it be enough to get you where you want to go?

## March 26

*"You don't get paid for the hour. You get paid for the value you bring to the hour."*
Jim Rohn

Many times we forget that most of us earn an income according to our knowledge and experience not just the time we put into something. I know in many cases we charge by time, but the truth is people want and need proper solutions and that means knowledge and experience which equals value. We all need to keep this in mind when we serve others in our vocation as well as social relationships. Be prepared to provide value in all you do!

## March 27

*"I have no special talents.
I am only passionately curious."*
Albert Einstein

I speak with many who say they have no real talent when in reality we all have been equipped with certain gifts, talents, skills and abilities. For some it may take a while to recognize or discover but we all have them. Curiosity is one thing that causes us to grow and improve. So feel free to ask questions, look for options and explore different opportunities. Hone your skills and improve your abilities and become the problem solver you are designed to become.

## March 28

*"As I grow older, I pay less attention to what men say.
I just watch what they do."*
Andrew Carnegie

It is high time you realize what you say must match what you do or else it is of no effect. The Good Book even says that a tree is known by its fruit. The old saying, "If you are going to talk the talk then you need to walk the walk" is correct. If you want people to accept you, be influenced by you, and follow your lead then being true to your word is vital.

## March 29

*"A person who never made a mistake
never tried anything new."*
Albert Einstein

What is one thing you've been waiting to try but haven't yet for some reason? Don't wait any longer, take that step and have faith. The reason most people never become extremely successful or do the extraordinary is because of fear. Do not allow fear to stop you from fulfilling your dreams and desires. Make a plan now to do that one thing you have dreamed about for years.

## March 30

*"First comes thought; then organization of that thought, into ideas and plans; then transformation of those plans into reality. The beginning, as you will observe, is in your imagination."*
Napoleon Hill

If you do not have an image in your mind of what you want or where you are going then it will be extremely difficult if not impossible to achieve. Begin today to get a picture of who you want to become, what you want to achieve and see yourself already there. Then you are on the road to achieving your goal.

## March 31

*"As a Man thinks in his heart, so is he."*
King Solomon

The heart is much more than just a pump that keeps our blood flowing. The heart is where our personal belief system resides. It is also where our will and emotions originate. Even God looks upon the heart to see what our real motives are. This is where we store up treasure for the harvest we desire. The treasure is what we allow to be stored in our heart because we will get a harvest based on the information we store there. Some people speak and think too much about sickness, disease, and death. Successful people talk and meditate more on health, wealth and happiness. What treasure are you storing?

## April 1

***"The difference between the possible and the impossible
lies in a person's determination."***
Tommy Lasorda

Determination is the driving force that makes most people
successful. The majority of people know exactly what
they need to do to achieve the life that they want, but
somehow they still aren't able to make it happen. The
biggest reason is they are too quick to give up trying.
Reaching your dreams is not easy, in fact, it's hard and
that's why most people fail to live the life they really want.
Be determined, don't procrastinate, live the life you want to
live.

## April 2

***"The pessimist sees difficulty in every opportunity. The
optimist sees the opportunity in every difficulty."***
Winston Churchill

Seeing the glass half full verses half empty could be very
important to your success. We must always be looking for
opportunities. I have found that when I encounter obstacles
or difficulties many times I find opportunities. I was told
long ago that if I trained my brain to always be looking for
the good in every situation and in every person I met I
would discover more opportunities than I ever thought
possible. Try it, it really works.

# April 3

### *"The difference between who you are and who you want to be is what you do."*
Bill Phillips

What you have to do to become what you want to be may not be pretty and it may not come easy. Everyone wants to become successful and significant. The fact is, what you do is a result of your outlook or perception and your perception is determined by what you allow to be fed into your mind. To quote it as Zig Zigler does, "Your <u>input</u> will determine your <u>outlook</u> and your outlook will determine your <u>output</u> and your output will determine your <u>destiny</u>." Therefore, to get where you really want to go you must put the right things into your mind and heart. If you don't already, start today to feed your mind the right stuff.

---

# April 4

### *"People create their own success by learning what they need to learn and then by practicing it until they become proficient at it."*
Brian Tracy

The old saying "Practice makes perfect" is very true. For years I read books listen to CDs and attended seminars that gave me great information and advice, but I never put it into practice. The only way to get where you really want to go personally and professionally is to put what you learn into practice. I've heard for years that knowledge is power, but that isn't true. The only thing that will give you real power is "Action". Put what you know into action today!

## April 5

*"People were designed for accomplishment, engineered for success and endowed with seeds of greatness."*
Zig Ziglar

As the good book says, *"We are fearfully and wonderfully made."* As a human we are designed to succeed. We each are engineered with certain gifts, talents, skills and abilities. That's why some have natural inclinations to socialize, seek solitude, do things with their hands, communicate with words, express themselves through the different art forms, to lead, to follow, to calculate or to demonstrate which is all part of their makeup. You are made to fulfill a purpose in this life so use what you have been given and be the success for which you were intended.

## April 6

*"Whatever the mind can conceive and believe, the mind can achieve."*
Napoleon Hill

The formula for success is simple: Belief + Behavior = Results. What you believe will determine the choices you make and the actions you take. We all want results in our life, but if you are not getting the results you desire something must change. The thing that must change is your behavior but as a human you cannot change your behavior until you change what you believe. Therefore, build your personal belief system with the things that are true and accurate and experience the results you desire.

## April 7

### *"What we think, we become."*
Prince Gautama Siddharta

Physiologists tell us that our lives will go in the direction of our most predominant thoughts. So what are you thinking about? Think on the positive not the negative. Another reason to think positively not negatively is your thoughts can also determine how you feel. You can't get angry without first having an angry thought or happy without first having a happy thought. You can only hold one thought at a time so make every thought count. Control your thought-life and you control your destiny.

## April 8

### *"Your attitude, not your aptitude, will determine your altitude."*
Zig Ziglar

Attitude is a funny thing, it not only determines where you go in life, but it can also determine how fast you get there. The first thing you notice about someone with a positive attitude is normally a smile. That smile is powerful, it is magnetic. Medical science says when you smile a hormone is released that strengthens your immune system. They also discovered that same hormone is released in anyone who sees you smile. So you have the ability to not only help yourself but everyone with whom you come in contact. Practice a positive attitude everyday!

## April 9

*"The problem with motivation
is the one who needs motivating is the one
with total responsibility for achieving it"*
Donny Ingram

We each are responsible for our own motivation. Therefore, whatever it takes, listening to certain CDs, reading quotes, or reminding yourself with notes, just do it. It must be done continually to maintain a level of motivation needed to succeed.

## April 10

*"Don't wait for the perfect moment,
take the moment and make it perfect"*
Unknown

Every moment of every day we have a choice. We can either focus on the negative or the positive. Something good can be found in every situation, every circumstance, every trial, every obstacle, or problem. It is a proven fact that positive and optimistic people live longer, happier and healthier lives. Take charge of your life and look for and expect the best in everything and everyone.

# April 11

***"What would you strive to accomplish if today's results were the only ones you would be remembered for?"***
Donny Ingram

The people who go down in history are those who give it all they've got every moment of every day. We all will be remembered for something so why not make it something great. Live everyday as if it were your last, complete every project and every assignment as though it was your final signature. You will be remembered by those you touch the most so let that memory be a seed of significance.

# April 12

***"Don't think outside the box.
Think like there is no box."***
Oprah Winfrey

You have probably heard the saying "Think outside the box" many times. I happened to like Oprah Winfrey's suggestion of thinking like there is no box. It's time we stop trying to fit today's issues into yesterday's mold. We need to explore new possibilities for success, new and more effective products and discover more avenues for meeting needs in today's marketplace. Start today to view every issue, every situation, and every product or service with an open and creative mind.

## April 13

*Prayer is not a "spare wheel" that you pull out
when in trouble, but it is a "steering wheel"
that directs the right path throughout life.*
Unknown

Some people only pray when a crisis arrives or tragedy hits
home. If we really believe in an all powerful, all seeing, all
knowing God then why wait until trouble arrives to talk
with Him. God can do nothing until we ask Him. So why
not allow him to drive your life instead of always using him
as a last resort to fix your problems? Have faith and give
Him control and watch the miracles begin to happen.

## April 14

*Why is a Car's WINDSHIELD so large & the Rear view
Mirror so small? Because our PAST is not as important
as our FUTURE. So, Look Ahead and Move on.*
Unknown

It really doesn't matter where you have been; it only
matters where you are going. Therefore, spend the
majority of your time focusing on today and the future not
yesterday.

## April 15

*"All things in life are temporary.*
*If going well, enjoy it, they will not last forever.*
*If going wrong, don't worry, they can't last long either."*
*Unknown*

Everything in life is constantly changing. Therefore, you must embrace it, love it, enjoy it and most of all be thankful for it.

## April 16

*Old Friends are Gold! New Friends are Diamond! If you get a Diamond, don't forget the Gold! Because to hold a Diamond, you always need a Base of Gold!*
Unknown

Those with whom you become friends are important to your future. Some will be with you only for a season, some for just a specific reason and some for a lifetime. Value each for his/her season and purpose and contribution into your life.

## April 17

***WORRYING does not take away tomorrow's TROUBLES; it takes away today's PEACE.***
George Eliot

As long as we live there will be troubles. We can minimize a great number of them through proper prior planning. My good friend and senior pastor Dr. David Rosier says, "Long term goals can prevent short term frustrations." Setting goals for your life can ease the need of worrying.

## April 18

***"Wherever you go, go there with all your heart."***
Todd Duncan

People who fail usually fail because they never really believe 100% in what they are doing and because of that their heart is really not in it. If it is worth attempting, it is worth giving it all your heart. Remember, belief plus behavior equals results.

## April 19

*"Every man is enthusiastic at times. One man has enthusiasm for thirty minutes, another for thirty days, but it is the man who has it for thirty years who makes a success in life."*
Edward B. Butler

I was told early in life that education breads confidence and confidence breeds enthusiasm which leads to success. Learn what you need to learn to be the best and watch how fast you become a success.

## April 20

*"Get excited and enthusiastic about your own dream. This excitement is like a forest fire – you can smell it, taste it, and see it from a mile away."*
Stephen Covey

If you have a dream or desire then you should be passionate about the process to get there. When you are passionate it's like a fire burning inside of you. As a great man once said, "When you're on fire, people will come from miles around just to watch you burn." Get excited!

## April 21

*"There is no sudden leap to greatness,*
*your success lies in doing, day by day."*
Max Steingart

Everyone wants to arrive overnight without any effort or discipline in their life. Sorry, but you must take it one day at a time and make every moment of every day count.

## April 22

*"The most valuable of all education is the ability to make*
*yourself do the thing you have to do when it has to be*
*done, whether you like it or not."*
Aldous Haxley

It is a hard lesson for most of us, but discipline is the key to achieving any goal. You must use discipline to your benefit and when you do, you'll start seeing progress in all you do.

## April 23

*"If you are going to achieve excellence in big things, you develop the habit in little matters. Excellence is not an exception, it is a prevailing attitude."*
Colin Powell

You must take PRIDE, Personal Responsibility In Developing Excellence, in everything you do, not just in the major things. Therefore, having an attitude of excellence will drive your success. Take PRIDE today!

## April 24

*"I have learned that success is to be measured not so much by the position that one has reached in life as by the obstacles that one has overcome while trying to succeed."*
Booker T. Washington

Some are able to reach certain positions because of family relationships or inheritances. Most all others who achieve real success had to overcome many obstacles along the way. Those are the ones who receive admiration and appreciation from many followers.

## April 25

***"The block of granite which was an obstacle in the pathway of the weak becomes a stepping-stone in the pathway of the strong."***
Thomas Carlyle

Don't allow what may appear to be a major obstruction to hinder you from achieving your dreams. Use every hurdle to learn and grow.

## April 26

***"Adversity causes some men to break; Others to break records."***
William A. Ward

You can use what is meant to break you to propel you into your destiny. Never allow any stumbling block whether it is mental or physical to slow you down and hinder you from achieving your goals.

## April 27

***"Remember, man does not live on bread alone:***
***sometimes he needs a little buttering up."***
John C. Maxwell

Being nice is extremely powerful.  It will disarm angry people; it can open the door for opportunities as well as help create and build relationships.  Be nice and show you care about others and watch what happens.

## April 28

***"People have a way of becoming what***
***you encourage them to be – not***
***what you nag them to be."***
Scudder N. Parker

People respond differently; some to words of affirmation, others to your time and attention, some to gifts and opportunities, and others to acts of service.  All of which are encouraging actions.  Use every opportunity to encourage those you come into contact with today and every day.

## April 29

*"Pretend that every single person you meet has a sign around his or her neck that says, 'Make me feel important.' Not only will you succeed in sales, you will succeed in life."*
Mary Kay Ash

Everyone wants to feel valuable and significant. When you can provide this feeling, you will win with everyone, especially those you deal with every day. It doesn't cost a nickel, so make everyone you meet feel special and experience how you become a magnet for success.

## April 30

*"Carve your name on hearts and not on marble."*
Charles H. Spurgeon

Be concerned more with people than positions. Seek to influence and help others rather than climb the corporate latter and you will encounter true success.

## May 1

*"Real generosity is doing something nice
for someone who will never find out."*
Frank A. Clark

When you are able to touch people's lives in ways that only benefit them you become a true blessing to the world. I like the philosophy of Peter Lowe, "If you're going to err, err on the side of generosity." In doing so, you'll always win.

## May 2

*"The way to happiness: Keep your heart free from hate,
you mind from worry, live simply, expect little, give much,
scatter sunshine, forget self, and think of others."*
Norman Vincent Peale

We are not promised happiness, but we can create happiness in ourselves as well as others by doing the simple things: Giving, loving, sharing, caring and inspiring others.

## May 3

*"Four short words sum up what has lifted most successful individuals above the crowd: A LITTLE BIT MORE. They did all that was expected of them and a little bit more."*
A. Lou Vickery

People who have a history of winning and succeeding have one thing in common – They go above and beyond and give a little bit more than the competition. Give it a try!

## May 4

*"Do your duty and a little bit more, and the future will take care of itself."*
Andrew Carnegie

Never pass the buck, or point a finger. Take responsibility and ownership and watch your future come together. No one can do it like you can!

## May 5

*"There are no traffic jams along the extra mile."*
Roger Staubach

In today's marketplace the majority of people ignore things they think aren't their responsibility. People who achieve success take ownership and complete task that need to be done regardless of whose job it is. Be that person!

## May 6

*"Success is to be measured not by wealth, power, or fame, but by the ratio between what a man is and what he might be."*
H.G. Wells

There is so much more that can be accomplished if only we could see that we can do it. Don't fall short of your goals, your career or you life by limiting yourself. Take a step back and look at what you really are designed to do.

## May 7

***"Start by doing what's necessary; then do what's***
***possible; and suddenly you are doing the impossible."***
Saint Francis of Assisi

Nothing is impossible if you truly unite your mind, body
and soul and let your passion drive you. People said the
four minute mile couldn't be broken, but it was. They said
we would never achieve flight, but we did. We were never
supposed to land on the moon, but we did. I was never
supposed to finish college or write books according to my
family and teachers, but I did. Never listen to anyone who
says, "It can't be done"!

## May 8

***"Rule No. 1: Use your own good judgment in all***
***situations. There will be no additional rules."***
Employee handbook, Nordstrom department store

Some say that common sense is not so common anymore.
Prove them wrong. Use your intelligence and make good
choices.

## May 9

***"People, even more than things, have to be restored,***
***renewed, revived, reclaimed, and redeemed;***
***never throw out anyone."***
Audrey Hepburn

You have the ability and I believe the responsibility to inspire those around you to believe in themselves. You can be the influence they need to reach higher and achieve more than they ever thought possible.

---

## May 10

***"One of the hardest tasks of leadership is***
***understanding that you are not what you are,***
***but what you're perceived to be by others."***
CEO of Florida Steel

Perception is reality. What others believe about you is true for them. Therefore, be aware of how others perceive you, your leadership, your values, your morals and your integrity. You are the only one who can change you!

## May 11

*"The three great essentials to achieve anything worth while are, first, hard work; second, stick-to-itiveness; third, common sense."*
Thomas Edison

These three will take you all the way to your goals. Put them to work in your life and career and help others to do the same.

## May 12

*"A positive attitude may not solve all your problems, but it will annoy enough people to make it worthwhile."*
Unknown

Being positive is way under-rated today. Not only having a positive attitude but maintaining one is the one factor that will pave the way for more promotions, opportunities, contacts, appointments and sales. Get up every morning and put yours in gear.

## May 13

*"If you want to change the fruits, you will first have to change the roots. If you want to change the visible, you must first change the invisible."*
T. Harv Eker

For every action there is a reaction. Nothing happens on its own. There is always unseen activity before we can enjoy the change in the natural. If you want to see something different on the outside then you must have a change on the inside.

## May 14

*"Never look back on the past; you might trip over the future."*
JoAnna DeLuna

I like to keep a journal of my life and work and I recommend it for everyone. However, I don't recommend continually looking back to see what happened in the past. Knowing that is great but you must spend most of your time focusing on the necessities for today and your path for the future.

## May 15

*"Never underestimate the power of your actions.
One small gesture can change a person's life,
for better or for worse."*
Donny Ingram

Recognize the power of influence you have on those around you. Take every opportunity to be the inspiration and motivation to uplift and encourage others. Be the CAO "Chief Attitude Officer" of your organization.

## May 16

*"We experience joy in life by the words we speak."*
Proverb

Your words carry more power than you may think. What you say can either build or destroy people. Use your words very carefully and always be positive even in a negative situation. Always be looking for the good not the bad!

## May 17

### *"If you do the work you get rewarded. There are no shortcuts in life."*
Michael Jordon

Michael Jordan missed more than 9000 shots in his career. He lost almost 300 games, 26 times. He was trusted to take the game winning shot and missed. He said "I have failed over and over and over again in his life. And that is why I succeed." Your key to success is no different. Never quit, keep working for what you want to achieve!

## May 18

### *"The environment you fashion out of your thoughts, your beliefs, your ideals, your philosophy is the only climate you will ever live in."*
Dr. Stephen Covey

Be firm in your beliefs, be willing to stand for your values and always keep your thoughts positive. We are told that our thought-life will determine the direction we travel, the decisions we make and ultimately the success we are able to achieve. Think good thoughts!

69

## May 19

*"I am still determined to be cheerful and happy in whatever situation I may be; for I have also learned from experience that the greater part of our happiness or misery depends upon our dispositions and not upon our circumstances."*
Martha Washington

I love the saying, "This too shall pass." We need to realize that what we focus on will determine our state. No matter how difficult the situation you will survive and you will be better for it!

## May 20

*"Even a mistake may turn out to be the one thing necessary to a worthwhile achievement."*
Henry Ford

Down through history great people have always made mistakes. A mistake leads you a little closer to success. According to some writers Thomas Edison had 9,999 mistakes before inventing the light bulb. But many of them lead to other great discoveries. So learn from your mistakes and use them to further your progress toward your goal.

## May 21

*"Few will have the greatness to bend history itself; but
each of us can work to change a small portion of events,
and in the total of all those acts will be written
the history of this generation."*
Robert F. Kennedy

What part will you change?  Make the commitment today
to change what you can for the better and don't worry
about the things you cannot.   Your changes can make
history for everyone involved.

## May 22

*"You are, at this moment, standing, right in the middle of
your own acres of diamonds."*
Earl Nightingale

Some people are so busy looking for something greater that
they miss the opportunities right in front of them.  You can
enjoy all that life has to offer by just taking advantage of
the things that most never see.

## May 23

*"The last of the human freedoms is to choose one's attitude in any given set of circumstances."*
Victor Frankl, M.D.

Attitude is a funny thing, it's the only thing we have total control over. Do your absolute best to maintain a positive attitude. It takes practice day in and day out but by doing so you will become a magnet for success.

## May 24

*"Money is the most envied, but the least enjoyed. Health is the most enjoyed, but the least envied."*
Charles Caleb Colton

As long as you have your health, you can earn more money. Keep your priorities in order and take care of number one. Eat healthy, exercise often and fill your mind with motivational and inspirational information.

## May 25

*"Look behind you.  If no one is following, it's a pretty good clue that you are not leading well."*
Ron Marks

Lead with confidence, boldness, care and passion.  This will insure you have followers. More importantly your leadership will lead them to greater achievement and victory.

## May 26

*"If you can't excel with talent, triumph with effort."*
Dave Weinbaum

The folks who are always coming out on top and enjoying success are not always the most talented.  They are not the most educated nor have the most resources.  They are the determined.   And as Babe Ruth once said, "It's hard to beat someone who refuses to give up."

## May 27

*"The Noah rule:  Predicting rain doesn't count;
building arks does."*
Warren Buffett

There is always someone who wants to tell you how it will
not work, what is wrong with the system or why it can't be
done.  Never pay attention to them, start doing what you
know needs to be done.

## May 28

*"You have to 'be' before you can 'do,' and do
before you can 'have.'"*
Zig Ziglar

You can't do brain surgery without first being educated to
do it.  You'll never enjoy the fruits of this life without first
being a person of character, integrity, and commitment.

## May 29

*"The strength of a nation lies in the homes of its people."*
Abraham Lincoln

The state of America or any country for that matter can be accredited to the condition of the marriages, the family relationships and the finances in the homes of their citizens. As you work today, I encourage you to try and influence every person in every transaction or conservation to step up and take responsibility to live a life of purpose.

## May 30

*"An investment in knowledge always pays the best interest."*
Benjamin Franklin

Remember, knowledge produces confidence and confidence produces enthusiasm and enthusiasm sells. If it cost you all you have, get the knowledge you need to live your life to its fullest.

## May 31

*"Nurture your mind with great thoughts, for you will never go any higher than you think."*
Benjamin Disraeli

Ever heard the old saying, "If you think you can or you think you can't, you're right" Your thoughts produce actions and your actions determine where you go and how fast you get there. Think right thoughts! You can only hold one at a time so make it count.

---

## June 1

*"Be the change you want to see in the world."*
Mahatma Gandhi

You may not be able to change the whole world, but you can change the world for one person at a time. Don't miss an opportunity to influence change in a positive way.

# June 2

## *"For he who has health has hope; and he who has hope, has everything."*
Owen Arthur

It always amazes me to hear healthy people giving excuses for not being able to do certain things. Yet I look around and see others with tremendous health issues or disabilities doing phenomenal things. If you are healthy then enjoy your health and always be positive.

# June 3

## *"Success usually comes to those who are too busy to be looking for it."*
Henry Thoreau

Some people are so busy trying to make the next step up the latter that they neglect the things that would assure them of promotion. Take care of the little things and the big things will come much easier.

## June 4

*"What we think determines what happens to us, so if we want to change our lives, we need to stretch our minds."*
Wayne Dyer

Zig Zigler once said, "Your input will determine your outlook and your outlook will determine your output and your output will determine your destiny." It all starts with our thinking. Control your thought life and you control your future.

## June 5

*"With greater confidence in yourself and your abilities, you will set bigger goals, make bigger plans, and commit yourself to achieving objectives that today you only dream about."*
Brian Tracy

Never place limits on yourself. Obtain confidence through knowledge of yourself. Dream big and put a plan in place to achieve your dreams.

## June 6

***"If you're not prepared to be wrong,***
***you'll never come up with anything original."***
Sir Ken Robinson

Everyone is wrong at times. The key however is not to fear being wrong or allowing fear to stop you from taking actions to try something new. Fear, as my good friend Jeff Cook always told me, is just **F**alse **E**vidence **A**ppearing **R**eal.

## June 7

***"Motivation is a fire from within.***
***If someone else tries to light that fire under you,***
***Chances are it will burn very briefly."***
Dr. Stephen Covey

Others can only motivate you for a short time. Internal motivation is a must for success. Mr. Zig Zigler says, "Motivation doesn't last, but neither does bathing, that's why we need it often." Find that motivation in yourself and turn it on everyday.

## June 8

***"You can never earn in the outside world***
***more than you earn in your own mind."***
Brian Tracy:

How much do you value your skills, talent, and abilities? Most people underestimate their value and sell themselves short. Determine what you want, what it will take to get it and go for it.

## June 9

***"One-half of life is luck; the other half is discipline —***
***and that's the important half, for without discipline you***
***wouldn't know what to do with luck."***
*Carl Zuckmayer*

I've always been told that luck is just preparedness meeting opportunity. That being true all you must do is be disciplined to take advantage of every opportunity that comes your way.

## June 10

*"We must always change, renew, rejuvenate ourselves; otherwise we harden."*
Johann Wolfgang von Goethe

If you are not changing, you are not growing. Always be ready to change your approach to matters and renew your mind with positive thoughts. Don't conform to the same old way of doing business. Be creative! Seek out the new and improved!

## June 11

*"The whole purpose of education is to turn mirrors into windows."*
Sydney J. Harris

Education will help you see the possibilities that exist. It doesn't have to be formal. Be willing and open to learning new things every day. Step outside your comfort zone and excel.

## June 12

*"Every adversity, every failure, every heartache carries with it the seed on an equal or greater benefit."*
Napoleon Hill

Every struggle, difficulty or obstacle that you face in life has within it the potential for you doing even greater things than you thought possible.   Face them with eyes for opportunities.

## June 13

*"The quality, not the longevity, of one's life is what is important."*
Dr. Martin Luther King Jr.

What determines your quality of life?   Some think money, relationships or government.   Actually, the one thing that will determine quality is the meaning you give to everything that you encounter.   Always look for the positive!

## June 14

*"The purpose of learning is growth,*
*and our minds, unlike our bodies,*
*can continue growing as we continue to live."*
Mortimer Adler

Use every situation and circumstance to learn and grow. Never stop filling your mind with positive, inspirational and encouraging material. You will enlarge you boundaries tremendously.

## June 15

*"If you do not conquer self,*
*you will be conquered by self."*
Napoleon Hill

The person most of us have more difficulty with than any other is self. That's why you should always be talking to yourself, telling yourself what you want to see happen. You must do it continually because repetition is the mother of success.

# June 16

*"You and I are essentially infinite choice-makers. In every moment of our existence, we are in that field of all possibilities where we have access to an infinity of choices."*
Deepak Chopra

What makes the human creature different from all other creatures born on this planet is our ability to choose. Always weigh the benefits in every decision and make the best choice.

# June 17

*"Eventually we all have to accept full and total responsibility for our actions, everything we have done, and have not done."*
Hubert Selby Jr., Requiem for a Dream

If there is one thing needed more than ever in the times we live is for people to take responsibility for their actions. If you're a leader and manager you obviously already do but you must also stress this to everyone under your influence.

## June 18

*"Wise sayings often fall on barren ground,*
*but a kind word is never thrown away."*
Arthur Helps

Never underestimate the power of a kind word. It provides a feeling of being loved and valued. You will be remembered not for what you did or even what you said but for the feeling it gave others.

## June 19

*"The great organizations of the country and the great lives in history have been built on the answers to 'why?' You can teach someone how to do a task, but that doesn't assure his doing it. But let him discover why and he'll learn how in spite of all obstacles. The key is not how to live, but why you are living."*
Charlie "Tremendous" Jones

Ask yourself "Why" every day. Why am I here, why do I do the work I do, why, why, why? When you know the why you hold the power to achievement.

## June 20

***"I believe that one of the most important habits
for us to cultivate is to find something positive
in everything that happens."***
Charlie "Tremendous" Jones

When you look for the good in everything you initiate the positive thinking process. When you look to find a way that you can make it better you initiate the creative thinking process which re-enforces the positive thinking process. Before long you have trained your brain to be positive.

## June 21

***"The great mystery isn't that people do things badly but
that they occasionally do a few things well. The only thing
that is universal is incompetence. Strength is always
specific! Nobody ever commented, for example, that the
great violinist Jascha Heifetz probably couldn't play the
trumpet very well."***
Peter Drucker

Don't worry about your weaknesses, work on your strengths, people will remember you for what you do well not what you can't do.

# June 22

### *"Kites rise highest against the wind...*
### *Not with it."*
Winston Churchill

Success doesn't come easy. Sometime you must go against the grain and against the current thought process to introduce new avenues and actions for organizational success. Never be afraid of introducing a new idea or product that will benefit the efficiency, the effectiveness or the bottom line.

# June 23

### *To Be Your Best, Try Being "Uncomfortable"*
Todd Wilms

Being comfortable with the world around us makes us lazy, removes stimulation, and hinders our motivation. On the other hand, being uncomfortable forces us to be creative and resolve the discord. "Uncomfortable" motivates and clarifies our direction. It gives us insight into the problems around us and many times our very best innovations come from those very uncomfortable places.

## June 24

*"If you watch a guy who's moving up, you'll see one who knows that he deserves nothing and owes everything. But when he gets to the place that he decided he owes nothing and deserves everything, he will be on his way down before he knows what happened."*
Charlie "Tremendous" Jones

Always be thankful for what you have and keep a spirit of gratitude for where you are today. So many get to a great position and then lose it due to arrogance and pride. Never let that happen to you.

## June 25

*"The man on top of the mountain didn't fall there."*
Anonymous

Achieving success is not easy; it takes work and most of the time lots of it. However, you must keep in mind that nothing or no one can hold you back except you. Give it all you have today!

## June 26

> *"Don't be afraid of being scared. To be afraid is a sign*
> *of common sense. Only complete idiots*
> *are not afraid of anything."*
> Carlos Ruiz Zafón

Fear is not always a bad thing. Some things should scare us, but don't let it stop you from attempting to reach for greater things or setting goals that some say are unreachable. You can do most anything if you believe and put your mind to it.

## June 27

> *"We are all put in each other's lives*
> *to impact one another in some way,*
> *therefore, look for the GOOD in others."*
> Donny Ingram

This life is about relationships. The key is allowing the right relationships in your life. No one can achieve greatness on their own, it takes help. Appreciate those in your life and always be a blessing to them.

## June 28

### *"It is easier to go down the mountain than up, but the view from the top is the best."*
Unknown

The journey is always difficult, but once there the victory is sweet. Enjoy both because life is more about the journey than your destination.

## June 29

### *"If you want something you've never had you must do things that you've never done."*
Albert Einstein

I've been told many times that doing the same thing every day but expecting different results is insanity. If you really want more you must do things different than in the past. Be creative, bold and take the risk of stepping out of your comfort zone and going for it.

## June 30

### *"Nothing happens but first a dream."*
Carl Sandburg

Every successful person who has achieved something great first dreamed about it over and over. The one thing they did, however, is put action to their dreams. Go make it happen!

## July 1

### *"Getting over a painful experience is much like crossing monkey-bars. You have to let go at some point to move forward."*
C.S. Lewis

We all go through situations that sometimes really hurt us physically, emotionally or financially. The fact is you must forge ahead and let that hurt go or it will stunt your growth and hinder your efforts in reaching your goals.

## July 2

*"The quality of a person's life is in direct proportion to their commitment to excellence, regardless of their chosen field of endeavor."*
Vince Lombardi

You must take personal responsibility in developing excellence (PRIDE) in your life and work. Everyone is looking for success but too many fail to realize that success is a by-product of excellence. Set excellence as your standard and never waiver!

## July 3

*"Failure comes because we either thought and never took action or we took action without putting any thought into it."*
Donny Ingram

One of the main issues today in reaching goals and achieving certain positions is the lack of planning. Every goal must be thought out and a plan designed to reach that goal. Always plan for where you want to go in life and career.

## July 4

**"If there is a trait which does characterize leaders it is
opportunism. Successful people are very often those
who steadfastly refuse to be daunted by disadvantage
and have the ability to turn disadvantage to good effect.
They are people who seize opportunity and take risks.
Leadership then seems to be a matter of
personality and character."**
John Viney *Drive*

I'm proud our forefathers forged a new world and laid a
foundation that benefits all who call America home.
Celebrate freedom today and every day!

## July 5

*"Learn to set your course by the stars,
not by the lights of every passing ship."*
General Omar Bradley

Focus your thoughts and your actions on where you are
headed. Never allow others to hinder or stop your journey
to victory.

## July 6

*"The world has a habit of making room for the person
whose words and actions show that they
know where they're going."*
Napoleon Hill

Be committed, bold and above all be positive in your labors
to achieve your goals. Doors open for people who exhibit
these behaviors.

## July 7

*"The gem cannot be polished without friction, nor the
man perfected without trials."*
Chinese Proverb

It is the difficulties we face, the obstacles we encounter and
the pain we experience that hones us and prepares us for
victory. Use what you have experienced to propel you into
greatness.

## July 8

*"Unless you try to do something beyond what you have already mastered, you will never grow."*
Ronald E. Osborn

The key to growth is of course stretching ourselves past anything we have done in the past. Set higher goals and expect to achieve them. You can do it!

## July 9

*"Give the world the best you have and the best will come back to you."*
Madeline Bridges

You will never fail to receive when you have given your best. I like what the apostle Paul said and I paraphrase, "What you do for others God will do for you." This is a law of life. Live it!

## July 10

*"Knowledge is like climbing a mountain; the higher you reach, the more you can see and appreciate."*
Unknown

You should use every opportunity to learn something even if it is what not to do. The more you know the better quality decisions you can make and you will be healthier, happier and more prosperous.

## July 11

*"The law of Use or Lose. This law says that if you're not using what you have, you're losing it. If you're using what you have, you're getting more of it."*
Charlie "Tremendous" Jones

Never stop using what you have learned over your life. Even if it is playing an instrument and no one wants to listen. Play to yourself. Stay sharp and always be honing your skills.

## July 12

*"Learn as if you were going to live forever,*
*live as if you were going to die tomorrow."*
Mahatma Gadhi

Never think that you are too old to grow. Learning is growing and we should never stop. Use everything you have to live life to its fullest. None of us are promised tomorrow.

## July 13

*"The best way to succeed is to discover what you love*
*and find a way to offer it to others."*
Oprah Winfrey

Your passion for what you do will draw the attention of others and cause them to want what you have. Be prepared to give it as often as possible.

## July 14

### *"Win without boasting.  Lose without excuses."*
Vince Lombardi

I like the philosophy of the great football coach, Bear Bryant, "If we win, they did it.  If we lose, I did it."  No one likes egotism or blamers.

## July 15

### *"Excuses are the nails used to build a house of failure."*
Don Wilder

When you give excuses it never sounds positive.  Always try to put a positive spin on negative situations.  Even if the experience is negative, turn it around.

## July 16

*"Customer service is not a department it's an attitude."*
Mac Anderson

The great customer service consults today tell us if we want our company to not only grow but have sustained growth we must provide good customer service. Again the main factor is having a positive attitude.

## July 17

*"Live your life each day as you would climb a mountain. An occasional glance toward the summit keeps the goal in mind, but many beautiful scenes are to be observed from each new vantage point. Climb slowly, steadily, enjoying each passing moment; and the view from the summit will serve as a fitting climax for the journey."*
Harold V. Melchert

Enjoy the journey in your life and career. Take every opportunity to stop and smell the roses along the way. You'll be happier for doing so!

## July 18

*"All that is expected of us today is that we give our best."*
Donny Ingram

To earn top rewards in life and career you must get up every morning and make the decision to give 100% in everything you attempt. Nothing more and nothing less will get you where you want to go. Give it your best today!

## July 19

*"What people say, what people do, and what they say they do are entirely different things."*
Margaret Meade

Make sure you follow through with all your promises. People will respect, follow and give their business to those who do what they say they will do. Be that person!

## July 20

*"The indispensable first step to getting the things you want out of life is this: decide what you want."*
Ben Stein

The steps to achieving what you want are very simple. The first is knowing what it is you really want. If you don't know then sit down and start writing down some things you want. It may take several days but keep adding until you get several. Then START!

## July 21

*"The best way to find yourself,
is to lose yourself in the service of others."*
Mahatma Ghandi

We said several days ago that life is about relationships and that is true. It is also about serving those who are in relationship with you. Keep a servants heart and you'll experience greatness in the eyes of many.

## July 22

***"Leadership is the capacity and will to rally men
and women to a common purpose and the character
which inspires confidence."***
Bernard Montgomery
British Field Marshall

People want to follow someone who is confident.  They are looking for the leader who knows where he or she is going and has a plan to get there.  Be that leader!

## July 23

***"Nearly all men can stand adversity, but if you want to
test a man's character, give him power."***
Abraham Lincoln

Many leaders have learned this the hard way.  They promoted people who did not know how to handle the power of their position.  Know the character of those you hire and promote.

## July 24

### *"God grant that men of principle shall be our principal men."*
Thomas Jefferson

Always vote for and promote people who stand for good values and have a record of living and working with integrity. A good test is to learn about their past, what they have done and how they have stood by their principles. This will tell the story!

## July 25

### *"Successful leadership is not about being tough or soft, sensitive or assertive, but about a set of attributes. First and foremost is character"*
Warren Bennis

Great leaders put others first and foremost when setting plans and making decisions. A person of great character is always thinking of others. Be that leader!

## July 26

*"Leadership is learning to give whether you get anything or not! If you ever give something to get something, you're not giving in the true sense of the word, you're trading!"*
Charlie "Tremendous" Jones

The greatest teacher of all time, Jesus, taught that in order to receive you must give first. He also taught that we must give out of a heart of love. As a leader your first priority should be giving and serving those you are leading.

## July 27

*"In the last analysis, what we are communicates far more eloquently than anything we say or do."*
Stephen Covey

You must be before you can do. Who you are as a person will determine what others think about you. If you want to draw business and be a great leader of people it has to start with who you really are inside.

## July 28

### *"Mountaintops inspire leaders,*
### *but valleys mature them."*
Winston Churchill

Everyone wants to climb that mountain and get to the top of their industry. How long you are able to stay there is determined by what you learn and master on your way up.

## July 29

### *"The highest reward for man's toil is not what he gets for*
### *it but what he becomes by it."*
John Ruskin

There has been far too many who have worked their way up the corporate latter and in doing so became hard, cruel and ungrateful. Achieving success will change you, but let it be for the better.

## July 30

*"People do not follow uncommitted leaders. Commitment can be displayed in a full range of matters to include the work hours you choose to maintain, how you work to improve your abilities, or what you do for your fellow workers at personal sacrifice."*
Stephen Gregg
Chairman and CEO of Ethix Corp.

Commitment is a big word and requires a sacrifice of time, talent and resources. True leaders are easy to spot because of their commitment.

## July 31

*"Commitment is the enemy of resistance, for it is the serious promise to press on, to get up, no matter how many times you are knocked down."*
David McNally

As a great baseball player once said, "It's hard to beat someone who will not give up." Let that be said of you!

## August 1

*"Just remember that if you're not working at your game to the utmost of your ability, there will be someone out there somewhere with equal ability who is. And one day you'll play each other, and he'll have the advantage."*
"Easy" Ed Macauley
as told by Bill Bradley

Being the best may require hours and hours of practice and study. One great NBA player who was named MVP after the National Championship stated, "Every day I go out, I require more of myself than any player, any fan or any coach could possibly ask." That's what made him great and it will do the same for you.

## August 2

*"Nothing is easier than saying words. Nothing is harder than living them day after day."*
Arthur Gordon

Our words are powerful. As a leader, manager or employee always, and I mean always, live by your words. As the good book says, "By your words you will be justified, and by your words you will be condemned."

## August 3

*"Desire is the key to motivation, but its determination and commitment to an unrelenting pursuit of your goal - a commitment to excellence - that will enable you to attain the success you seek."*
Mario Andretti

Decide today how much you really desire to achieve your goals?   It will take determination and commitment to succeed.  Are you prepared?

## August 4

*"In order to 'hold fast' to something, one must allow oneself to be held to something. That commitment may be one of the hardest things to practice in a world of so much choice."*
Sheena Iyengar

Once again, the key to success is knowing what you want, why you want it and setting a plan of action to get there. The WHY is the key, that why must be powerful or you will never do whatever it takes to get it.  Of course, it must be legal, moral and ethical.

## August 5

*"Leaders who make it a practice to draw out the thoughts and ideas of their subordinates and who are receptive even to bad news will be properly informed. Communicate downward to subordinates with at least the same care and attention as you communicate upward to superiors."*
L. B. Belker

If you want to be heard and respected, then you must listen and respect others, especially those who are following your leadership. Be a leader who cares!

## August 6

*"Regardless of the changes in technology, the market for well-crafted messages will always have an audience."*
Steve Burnett

Practice what you need to say and how you need to say it. Especially when using the written word. Most of all, never repeat anything you are not willing to sign your name to.

## August 7

*"Talkers have always ruled. They will continue to rule.*
*The smart thing is to join them."*
Bruce Barton
Congressman and Author

Without words very little will get accomplished. Be one who is able to communicate verbally. Most of all make sure your message has value.

## August 8

*"No person was ever honored for what he received.*
*Honor has been the reward for what he gave."*
Calvin Coolidge

Always be a giver. Be willing to give of your time, talent and skill to service the common good, the good of your team, your company and your community. You'll never be forgotten for being a giver.

## August 9

***"You will discover that you have two hands.
One is for helping yourself and
the other is for helping others."***
Audrey Hepburn

Every dollar you will ever earn will come from someone else. Therefore, by always serving others you will be a winner in life.

---

## August 10

***"Motivation is the ultimate root of success."***
Geoffrey James

I agree with Omar Periu that the following ten actions will help you to become insanely motivated:

- *C*ondition your mind to think positive thoughts.
- *C*ondition your body to have physical energy.
- *D*on't take negative people seriously.
- *A*lways be flexible.
- *A*ct with a higher purpose.
- *T*ake responsibility for your own results.
- *S*tretch past your limits every day.
- *D*on't wait for perfection; do it now!
- *E*at healthy.
- *H*ang around motivated people.

## August 11

### *"The secret to anyone's success is what I call "And-then-some syndrome."*
Carl Holmes

These three words separate the average from the top performers in any company. Top performers always do what is expected of them – **And Then Some**. Some call it the extra mile; others say it is going above and beyond. Whatever you want to call it really doesn't matter. What matters is putting it into action. Be an "And-then-some" performer.

## August 12

### *"Life is like a 10 speed bike, we all have gears we never use."*
Charles Schultz

We never really know what we can achieve until we are required to reach down and summon the courage to stretch our abilities and accomplish what we thought to be impossible. One more gear can make the difference. What can you achieve by shifting into another gear and applying a small amount of effort beyond what you normally do? Give it all you have today and enjoy the victory!

## August 13

*"Take the first step in faith.  You don't have to see the whole staircase, just take the first step."*
Dr. Martin Luther King Jr.

We all are often hesitant about stepping out to do something that we really are not confident in doing.  However, if you know in your heart that it is your desire, then have the faith to take the first step and watch the miracles begin to take place.  You can accomplish more than you ever thought possible.  Just believe!

## August 14

*"There is no elevator to success, you have to take the stairs."*
Jody Hedlund

Success doesn't come easy it takes effort.  Regardless of what you are attempting to accomplish it helps to be prepared for obstacles that arise on your journey.  Asking yourself questions can assist you in charting your course for victory.  Questions such as: What is my goal in achieving this task?  Why is it so important?  Will it require the help of others?  When should I complete this task and how long am I willing to work to reach this goal?  Plus many more, but you get the picture.  Prepare to succeed!

## August 15

### *"An arrow can only be shot by pulling it backward."*
Unknown

When life is dragging you back with difficulties, just imagine that it's going to launch you into something great. How you view your environment and circumstances will have an effect on where you are going and what you are able to achieve. Always be looking for the best, it doesn't matter what is happening now; the thought process for everyone should be: What is great about this and what can I do to make it better? Never give up!

## August 16

### *"Today will never come again. What will you do this day to be a blessing and a friend?*
Donny Ingram

Take time to encourage someone today. Take time to show that you care. Let your words heal and not wound. Our actions every day – big and small – should have the possibility of making a positive impact on the world around us. And we should be having a positive influence on everyone with whom we come in contact. Ignite everyone that you encounter today!

## August 17

*"It is not what you look at that matters,*
*it's what you see."*
Simple Truths

Vision is important, but focus is vital to success. I find that extremely successful people tend to think more positively about everything that happens. They try to focus on the positive in every situation and in every person with whom they come in contact. Focus on the good in your life today and experience how great the day can be.

## August 18

*"Triumph often is nearest*
*when defeat seems inescapable."*
B.C. Forbes

When everything seems impossible and you can feel failure just ahead is when you should stand your ground, do what you know is best, and let life take its course. Often times you will achieve victory by not allowing fear to take control and believing in yourself and your decisions. Never give up and always expect the best!

## August 19

*"In the confrontation between the stream and the rock,
the stream always wins… not through strength,
but by perseverance."*
H. Jackson Brown

The person who wins in life and career is not the one with more education, more experience, more resources, or more talent. The one who wins is the person who refuses to quit. The one who says, "If that doesn't work I'll try another avenue but **I WILL** find an answer or solution and achieve my goal. Never doubt that you are the best and you **CAN DO IT**!

## August 20

*"Sometimes in the winds of change
we find our true direction."*
Unknown

I have never met a person who loved change. Actually, change is not the problem; it is the transition that causes us pain. I have found not only in my own life but in the lives of many others that change can cause us to see new opportunities, new avenues for improvement and untapped potential in ourselves and those who are members of our team. Embrace change and expect to experience growth for yourself and others.

## August 21

*"Since we are destined to live out our lives*
*in the prison of our minds, our one duty is*
*to furnish it well"*
Peter Ustinov

What do you fill your mind with each day? I'm not talking about all you do in the process of your job. I'm talking about the spare time, maybe on your drive to and from work or the times where you just stop and vegetate for awhile. Remember, your thoughts will produce confidence and confidence produces actions and actions lead to your destiny. Therefore, fill your mind with thoughts of success, information that is motivational and educational. Listen to CDs or read material that inspires you and ignites a positive attitude. By doing so; you can experience a longer, healthier and far more prosperous life.

## August 22

*"The average pencil is seven inches long, with just a half-*
*inch eraser – in case you thought optimism was dead."*
Robert Brault

Look at the things around you and realize how creation is naturally optimistic. Always look for the obvious, not the hidden. Focus on the positive and do your best to avoid anything negative. Sometimes the people with whom we work and associate can be the most negative. However, they can be overcome with positivity. They may think you are crazy, but they will do one of two things; avoid you or get on board and quit being so pessimistic.

## August 23

*"You create opportunities by performing,*
*not complaining."*
Kamari aka Lyrikal

When you encounter people who are constant complainers how does it make you feel? You will always encounter them at work, social functions and even church. Never let their negativity infiltrate your mind and influence your behavior. You are a top performer and you must tell yourself that daily and re-enforce it with emotion. When you do this it will become reality in your life and doors will open that you never imagined possible.

## August 24

*"It's important to push yourself further than you think*
*you can go each and every day — as that is what*
*separates the good from the great."*
Kerri Strug

Athletes who break records, win championships and become icons for their sport and country have one thing in common. They consistently push themselves every day to lift more, jump higher, run faster, and do more than they did yesterday. One athlete said, "I demand more of myself than any coach, player or fan could possibly ask." That's what made him great! The same is true for anyone in any profession. You never know what you can accomplish until you push the boundaries and give it everything you have. Give it all you've got today and be great!

## August 25

*"If you will spend an extra hour each day
of study in your chosen field, you will be
a national expert in that field
in five years or less."*
Earl Nightingale

Do you have a special interest, something that really starts your engine? I believe we all have something that really hits home with us. If we put time and energy into learning all we can about that subject matter we will become an expert. Enough study and others begin to recognize you as an expert in that area. That is when doors of opportunity will open for you to increase your effectiveness and move on up.

## August 26

*"We are the music makers;
we are the dreamers of dreams...
We are the movers and shakers
of the world for ever, it seems."*
Arthur O'Shaughnessy

Leadership is what everyone is searching for so diligently. Leaders make things happen; they listen to others, discern what needs to be done, design plans of action and put them into motion. Everything rises and falls on leadership. If you don't think you are a leader, read Mark Sanborn's book "You don't need a title to be a leader." Now, become the leader you were designed to be!

## August 27

*"Thinking is easy, acting is difficult,
and to put one's thoughts into action
is the most difficult thing in the world."*
Johann Wolfgang von Goethe

Thinking without action is really just day dreaming. Acting on your thoughts requires effort, planning, resources and many times assistance from others. Therefore, unless you have the proper motivation to act you will never experience victory. Put those good thoughts into action today!

## August 28

*"You've got to visualize where you're headed and be very clear about it. Take a picture of where you're going to be in a few years."*
Sara Blakely

I'm reminded of the movie Caddy Shack where Chevy Chase says, "Be the ball." We must visualize ourselves achieving our goal before we actually arrive. In any sport we are told to visualize making the goal, sinking the putt or winning the race. I remember reading where one college basketball coach had half of his team to lay down around the goal and visualize hitting every free-throw. The other half practiced by shooting 100 free-throws each. After the experiment those visualizing the shot had a much better percentage than those who actually practiced. Visualize where you want to go and what you want to achieve today.

## August 29

*"The more we give love,*
*the greater our capacity to do so."*
Dr. David Hawkins

Everyone desires to be loved. According to one study, the number one reason for a poor self-image in America is the lack of unconditional love. Whatever your occupation, age, gender or education you have the ability to give love. We show it in our expressions, words and our actions. The more we show the more we can show. Show love to everyone around you today.

## August 30

*"The best and most beautiful things cannot be seen or*
*touched - they must be felt with the heart."*
Helen Keller

When you view certain things you are stimulated with care, concern, love and sometimes pity. This is because your heart has been touched by something or someone that generates those feelings. Take note of how wonderful it is when your heart is touched in some way. Then be what touches the heart of others.

## August 31

### *"No matter what happens always be yourself."*
Dale Carnegie

Too many people try to mimic the actions of others. In our relationships both personal and professional, people want and need to see the real you. Therefore be yourself, no one can do it better than you. Don't worry if they like it or not. Just remember the SW3 principle, Some Will, Some Won't, So What!

## September 1

### *"To love what you do and feel that it matters... how could anything be more fun?"*
Katherine Graham

A leader has many qualities, but I feel the most important is passion. You cannot fake passion. It comes from inside and is fueled by your belief. When you believe in what you are doing it brings out your passion and you began to treasure every moment. You begin to experience a joy that others only dream about. Live your dream with passion and live life to its fullest.

## September 2

*"Nobody is perfect, and nobody deserves to be perfect. Nobody has it easy, everybody has issues. You never know what people are going through. So pause before you start judging, criticizing, or mocking others. Everybody is fighting their own unique war."*
Belinda Victoria Poltrino

We need to always remember that everyone is facing something, you may never know what it is, but you can be an inspiration not a critic. When you encounter people today, give them your best and let them see the good in you. Smile, laugh and be positive and watch how people light up in your presence.

## September 3

*"It's not what you gather, but what you scatter that tells what kind of life you have lived."*
Helen Walton

Life is really all about relationships. To become successful it takes more than just oneself. It means meeting, greeting and touching other people. In the end what we share and impart to others will measure how effective we were. We should be scattering encouragement, praise, laughter, kindness and care especially to those closest to us. Take advantage of the opportunities that come your way today and invest, impart and inspire people that cross your path.

## September 4

***"The basic building block of good communications is the feeling that every human being is unique and of value."***
Unknown

To really be understood and be taken seriously you must treat everyone with respect and care. Everyone wants to feel as though they are valuable and important. When you can effectively communicate that feeling to them they will give you their attention and their business.

## September 5

***"Don't find fault, find a remedy; anybody can complain"***
Henry Ford

At times we all want to blame someone else for difficult situations and circumstances. As a leader your focus should be finding solutions to the problems that arise. Don't worry about who did what or why just be a problem solver and you'll gain favor and encounter more opportunities than you can imagine.

## September 6

*"In this world people may throw stones in the path*
*of your success, it depends on you .....*
*What you make from them*
*a wall or a bridge."*
Unknown

Never fear what others do or say about you and your future.
Take everything that comes your way and make it work for
your good. The best revenge is massive success!

## September 7

*"What defines us is how well we rise*
*after falling."*
Lionel from Maid in Manhattan

There is no truer statement! Winners never stay down; they
rise to the occasion and fight until they are victorious.
Never be defeated, determine to get up and go at it again.

## September 8

### *"Optimism is the faith that leads to achievement"*
Helen Keller

Optimistic people see things from a different perspective. They are always looking for the best in every situation, every circumstance and in every person they meet. They not only discover greater opportunities, they live at a higher level, therefore, living healthier, happier and far more prosperous. Be more optimistic!

## September 9

### *"People may not remember what you do or even what you say, but they will never forget how you make them feel."*
Maya_Angelou

Life is all about feeling. The one thing that everyone wants is to feel valuable, needed and loved. When you can provide your customers, peers, associates and family that feeling, you have unlocked one of the major keys to success.

## September 10

***"Your own soul is nourished when you are kind;***
***it is destroyed when you are cruel."***
King Solomon

We all know or have known people who tend to treat others as being lower, less worthy, or stupid. This behavior will eventually destroy their health, wealth and joy. The old saying, "Honey will draw more flies than vinegar" is correct. Kindness not only sends a good message to others, but it improves you at the same time.

## September 11

***"You do not have a future.***
***You only have now."***
Asara Lovejoy

Most are working for the future and while that is not all bad it sometimes hinders us from enjoying and benefiting from the here and now. No one has the promise of tomorrow. Even though we should work and plan for the future we must live for today. Therefore, live this day as if it were your last and treat everyone as though you may never see them again. Success is yours!

## September 12

*"Too much thought and you miss the opportunity,*
*Not enough, and you spoil success."*
Rufus Tulio

Have you ever been told not to "over think" an issue? We should put some thought into the things we attempt because people acting without thinking brings on nightmares. On the other hand far too many over think and miss out on great opportunities. Think, but don't over-think!

## September 13

*"Too often we underestimate the power of a touch,*
*a smile, a kind word, a listening ear, an honest*
*compliment, or the smallest act of caring, all of which*
*have the potential to turn a life around."*
Leo F. Buscaglia

We never know what others are going through in their life. If we would but realize we have the power to change those around us with simple actions. Uplift someone today!

## September 14

*"If you don't design your own plan,*
*chances are you'll fall into someone else's plan.*
*And guess what they have planned*
*for you?  Not much."*
Jim Rohn

I have found that most people don't really have a plan for their life and career.  I mean they know what they want now or this year, but not long range.  If you don't have a plan you'll find yourself working to complete someone else's plan.  Take time to plan your future.

## September 15

*"The day soldiers stop bringing you their problems*
*is the day you have stopped leading them."*
General Colin Powell

Those who follow you will lean on you for advice and direction.  Always be aware of the needs of others and do your best to provide guidance that will benefit them.  Lead with care, compassion and boldness.

## September 16

***"Don't be afraid to go out on a limb…***
***That's where the fruit is."***
Mac Anderson

Sometimes when we step out we take a chance, but out there is where you'll discover your ability, skill and talent. Never be afraid to stand for what you think is right.

## September 17

***"Don't tell potential clients what you have done.***
***Show them what you can do for THEM."***
Patricia Fripp

Always be aware of what your customers, kids, friends and family are looking to gain. They are all listening to the same station, "WIIFM" What's In It For Me. When you can provide that you will not only win their confidence, but their business and loyalty.

## September 18

*"Don't aim for success if you want it;*
*just do what you love and believe in,*
*and it will come naturally"*
David Frost

Most people never think of themselves as successful. Don't focus on success, focus on what you enjoy doing and let your passion drive you. Success will then come to you!

## September 19

*"The greatest discovery you'll ever make,*
*is the potential of your own mind."*
Jose` Silva

Physiologists tell us by the time we graduate high school we have already set in our mind what we can and cannot achieve. However, we can change those set-points through education, experience and revelation knowledge. For most of us it starts with our attitude. Someone once said, "A bad attitude is like a flat tire, you can't go anywhere until you change it." Move those set-points in your mind. You can do far more than you think.

## September 20

*"Life is one big road with lots of signs. So when your riding through the ruts, don't complicate your mind. Flee from hate, mischief and jealousy. Don't bury your thoughts, put your vision to reality. Wake Up and Live!"*
Bob Marley

The key to achieving success in life is really following your heart. There may be something that you have had in the back of your mind for years and you have not attempted to step out and attempt it yet. Don't allow what others say or do stop you. Keep your thoughts positive and go do what you have longed to do for years.

## September 21

*"Learn from the mistakes of others — you can never live long enough to make them all yourself."*
John Luther

Andrew Carnegie once was asked, "What is the key to your success?" To which he replied, "Mistakes." He went on to say, "I try never to make the same one twice." We all are going to miss it now and then, but never let a mistake hold you back from achieving greatness.

## September 22

*"Great leadership usually starts with
a willing heart, a positive attitude,
and a desire to make a difference."*
Mac Anderson

Great leaders are those who really care. They care about
the well being and success of others as well as the
organization and it is evident in their actions, their words
and their plans. Be a great leader!

## September 23

*"Always laugh when you can.
It is cheap medicine."*
Lord Byron

Even the Bible says, "A merry heart doth good like a
medicine." In the world today it is sometimes hard to
laugh. However, it is good to see the humor in the things
that happens around us every day. Laughter is healing and
the more we laugh the better we feel and the more relaxed
others around us will become.

## September 24

*"Success is never owned, it's only rented
and the rent is due every day."*
Rory Vaden

Some only achieve success every now and again because their level of effort changes every day. To achieve the continual success that we each want and need we must put forth the same effort each day. Give it all you've got today and everyday!

## September 25

*"Success seems to be connected with action.
Successful people keep moving.
They make mistakes, but they don't quit."*
Conrad Hilton, Hilton Hotels

All through history we see that the people who achieved greatness and really made a difference were people who, even though failed many times, never quit going after their dream. Today is your day, make it count!

## September 26

*"Be willing to make decisions. That's the most important quality in a good leader. Don't fall victim to what I call the ready-aim-aim-aim-aim syndrome. You must be willing to fire."*
T. Boone Pickens

Making decisions is not difficult; making the right decisions is the issue. As a leader, it is your responsibility to take the information you can get and make the best decision possible. Don't worry; we will all miss it every now and again. The key is being willing to do it!

## September 27

*"The right man is the one who seizes the moment."*
Johann Wolfgang von Goethe

Opportunities are going to come your way continually. The key is being prepared to take advantage of those that will benefit you and others. Some call it lucky, but there is no such thing. Luck is just preparedness meeting opportunity.

## September 28

*"A man who has to be convinced to act
before he acts is not a man of action.
You must act as you breathe."*
Georges Clemmanceau

No one should have to convince you to do the right thing. Leaders take action to plan, prepare, expect and move in the direction that brings results. Be a person of action today!

## September 29

*"Try not to become a person of success, but rather try to become a person of value."*
Albert Einstein

Don't focus your efforts on being successful. Focus your efforts on becoming valuable to others. Success will be inevitable!

## September 30

### *"Truth is rarely given or received,*
### *but always revealed."*
Rufus Tulio

Never try to hide, cover up or ignore the real truth. It will come to light sooner or later. Truthful leaders may not always be popular, but they are forever respected and followed.

## October 1

### *"There comes a moment when you have to stop revving*
### *up the car and shove it into gear."*
David Mahoney

Some people are always planning, preparing and waiting for the "right" moment, which is not a bad thing. Don't try to be ready for everything or you'll never move forward. Be ready to move as soon as the opportunity presents itself!

## October 2

*"I would rather regret the things I have done
than the things I have not."*
Lucille Ball

Too many get to the end of their life and say, "I should have, I wish I had, or if I would have." Don't be that person. Step out and do what you have always wanted to do!

## October 3

*"If you don't make dust, you eat dust."*
Motto of Jack A. MacAllister

The key to achievement is moving forward. The status quo will get you no-where fast. Don't wait, get out front and lead others to success.

## October 4

*"Do not lie in a ditch, and say God help me; use the lawful tools He hath lent thee."*
English Proverb

We are all designed with certain traits and characteristics that help hone our skills, abilities and talents as we grow. Use what you have been given to accomplish task and achieve the goals you have set. Remember, you can do it!

## October 5

*"Most people spend more time planning their grocery shopping than designing their future."*
Unknown

To assure yourself of success you must take several steps.

1. Know what you want. Set goals!
2. Know why you want them. It must be powerful!
3. Take action, massive action.
4. Measure your progress continually.

Following these steps will take you where you want to go. You will be successful!

## October 6

***"Imagine how superficial our lives would be
if God didn't send circumstances that seem
disastrous for the moment but later prove
enriching and meaningful."***
Charlie "Tremendous" Jones

We may face situations that seem overwhelming but I have
realized that through those times I have grown and gained
valuable experience. Never give up, give in or give out.
All things are possible!

## October 7

***"The biggest disability is a negative attitude."***
Axel Ghinea

Some people never seem to realize that being negative
stunts their growth, hinders their success and causes good
people to avoid them. Don't be disabled, build a positive
attitude. In every situation or circumstance always think
positive!

## October 8

*"Luck comes to a man who puts himself in the way of it. You went where something might be found and you found something, simple as that."*
Louis L'Amour

You've already read this phrase several times but once again, "Luck is just preparedness meeting opportunity." You can only step through the doors of opportunity if you are prepared to do so. Be prepared and always be looking and expecting!

## October 9

*"There is no such thing in anyone's life as an unimportant day."*
Alexander Woollcott

Every day is an opportunity to touch someone's life, to influence a mind, or to help heal a broken heart. Value your day and show others how valuable they are to the world.

## October 10

*"A good plan implemented today is better than a perfect plan implemented tomorrow."*
George Patton

The key to achieving goals is implementation. Start moving toward success and measure your progress continually. If you're not making progress, then change your approach. Keep changing until you see improvement.

## October 11

*"Things may come to those who wait, but only things left by those who hustle."*
Abraham Lincoln

Those who are radically successful never wait around for things to happen. They go out and make things happen. The old saying, "If opportunity doesn't know, build a door" is correct. Go do it!

## October 12

***"What we think or what we know or what we believe is,
in the end, of little consequence,
The only consequence is what we do."***
John Ruskin

Action is the fuel to reaching your destiny.  To think, know and believe is great, but they will not propel you to accomplish you goals.  Start now to plan, prepare, expect and act on your goals.

## October 13

***"Ideas are a dime-a-dozen,
but those who put them into practice are priceless."***
Author Unknown

Leaders love to hear great ideas. But what they really appreciate are people who can take action to implement those great ideas.  Be a doer today!

## October 14

*"Creativity, as has been said, consists largely of rearranging what we know in order to find out what we do not know. Hence, to think creatively, we must be able to look afresh at what we normally take for granted."*
George Kneller

Two things are needed today. First, be able to look at every situation with a positive attitude and identify what is great. Second, be able to recognize what you can do to make it better. The first initiates the positive thinking practice and the second initiates the creative thinking process.

## October 15

*"Even if you're on the right track you'll get run over if you just sit there."*
Will Rogers

Headed in the right direction may have worked in the past, but today you must move with urgency. Be aggressive, determined and committed!

144

## October 16

### *"An idea is worthless unless you use it."*
John Maxwell

So many people have fantastic ideas, but they have no plan of implementation. Put action behind your good ideas and watch how it propels you forward.

## October 17

### *"Destiny is not a matter of chance, it is a matter of choice; it is not a thing to be waited for, it is a thing to be achieved."*
William Jennings Bryan

What has been on your mind and in your heart for month's maybe even years? It could possibly be connected to your purpose and your destiny. Don't wait, act on your passion and fulfill your destiny.

## October 18

*"No idea is so outlandish that it should not be considered with a searching but at the same time a steady eye."*
Winston Churchill

If you're like most of us you can look back over your life and recognize when you had a great idea but never followed through with it. Don't let another pass without acting and achieving great results.

## October 19

*"Success comes to the person who does today what you were thinking about doing tomorrow."*
Unknown

Success waits on no one. Don't procrastinate, if you can start today, do it! If you don't someone else may take your place.

## October 20

*"It's easy to come up with new ideas; the hard part is letting go of what worked for you two years ago, but will soon be out of date."*
Roger von Oech

The message here is change. If you are not changing you are dying. What worked well last year will not work as good this year. Always be looking for better, more effective and efficient methods.

## October 21

*"The best way to have a good idea is to have a lot of ideas."*
Dr. Linus Pauling

You may be one of those individuals who always has different ideas flowing through your mind. If so, write them down, research the possibilities and act on those that will benefit you, your company, and society.

## October 22

*"Everyone who's ever taken a shower has an idea. It's the person who gets out of the shower, dries off and does something about it who makes a difference."*
Nolan Bushnell

Again today, we are reminded that action is the key to succeeding. Put your great ideas to work and watch how you become, happier, healthier, and more prosperous.

## October 23

*"Don't wait for your ship to come in; swim out to it."*
Author Unknown

Far too many are waiting for something to happen to propel them into greatness. Never allow anything to hinder you from achieving success. Don't wait, go get it!

148

## October 24

*"You can't cross a sea by merely staring into the water."*
Rabindranath Tagore

Do you really want to achieve your goal, fulfill your purpose and reach your destiny?  Then stop dreaming about it and **DO IT**.

## October 25

*"Good character is more to be praised than outstanding talent. Most talents are to some extent a gift. Good character, by contrast, is not given to us. We have to build it piece by piece—by thought, choice, courage and determination."*
John Luther

Talent can only take you so far.  Character however, can carry you the remainder of the way.  Be a person of great character!

## October 26

### *"Anything worth doing is worth doing now!"*
Ralph Stayer

Procrastination is the greatest killer of success. Make a habit of doing what needs to be done immediately and experience the fast track to victory.

---

## October 27

### *"Once we rid ourselves of traditional thinking we can get on with creating the future."*
James Bertrand

Tradition causes many to miss opportunities for growth, achievement and recognition. Always be asking yourself "How can this be done better, more efficiently and effectively"? Be the change that is needed!

## October 28

*"The things we fear most in organizations—*
*fluctuations, disturbances, imbalances—*
*are the primary sources of creativity."*
Margaret J. Wheatley

In the middle of every difficulty there is an opportunity. The key is to find it and to be successful in doing so means keeping a positive attitude. Look for the opportunities and take advantage of every one.

## October 29

*"You don't drown by falling in the water;*
*you drown by staying there."*
Edwin Louis Cole

It doesn't matter how many times we fail. The key is to always get up and try it again. Remember, quitters never win and winners never quit.

## October 30

### *"Accept the challenges so that you may feel the exhilaration of victory."*
General George S. Patton, Jr.

Whatever challenge comes your way, stand and face it head-on. Remember, belief plus behavior equals results. Believe in yourself and act on that belief. You CAN overcome and win!

## October 31

### *"Let's make a dent in the universe."*
Steve Jobs

You were created for greatness. Don't worry about changing the entire world. Instead, be the influence in the world around you and change one life at a time.

## November 1

### *"Focus on what you can do,*
### *not on what you can't."*
Simple Truths

So often in life we're taught to work on our weaknesses instead of focusing totally on our strengths. Put your gifts, talents, skills and abilities to work for you and experience the best that life has to offer.

## November 2

### *"The secret to getting ahead is getting started.*
### *The secret of getting started is breaking your complex,*
### *overwhelming tasks into small manageable tasks,*
### *and then starting on the first one."*
Mark Twain

Walk down the street in any large city, look at the tall buildings, the massive companies and remember each one began with one thought. That thought was followed by action which resulted in success. Get started today!

## November 3

*"Everything you want is just outside your comfort zone."*
Robert Allen

Remember what Einstein said, "If you want something you've never had, you must do things you've never done." That means you must stretch yourself.

## November 4

*"If I had to sum up in a word what makes a good manager, I'd say decisiveness. You can use the fanciest computers to gather the numbers, but in the end you have to set a timetable and act."*
Lee J. Iacocca

Great leaders may be known for many things but the one thing that made them great is decision making. Make decisions based on fact and stand by your decision!

## November 5

### *"Fear is a reaction. Courage is a decision."*
Winston Churchill

Some say that courage is the absence of fear but that is not true. Courage is stepping out in the face of fear. Make the decision to be courageous.

## November 6

### *"One today is worth two tomorrows."*
Ben Franklin

None of us are promised tomorrow. Do all that you can do today to inspire, uplift and motivate those around you because you may not get another chance.

## November 7

***"If you can't feed 1,000 people, then feed one."***
Mother Teresa

Don't try to do more than you are allotted to do. You may not be able to change the world, but you can influence a change in those who cross your path each day.

## November 8

***"Whatever you do, or dream you can, begin it. Boldness has genius and power and magic in it."***
Johann Wolfgang von Goethe

Great men and women accomplish things because they are willing to start, passionate to continue and determined enough to succeed.

## November 9

### *"Without a sense of urgency, desire loses its value."*
Jim Rohn

Don't procrastinate, if you want it then go for it. Your desire will not get any stronger than it is in the moment.

---

## November 10

### *"Do not wait for life. Do not long for it. Be aware, always and at every moment, that the miracle is in the here and now."*
Marcel Proust

Today is the greatest opportunity you have to be bold, creative, grateful and successful. Don't waste a minute! Go ahead and be the leader, the motivator, the friend, the success you want to become. When you see it, others will also!

## November 11

### *"I have been impressed with the urgency of doing."*
Leonardo Da Vinci

Don't put off what you can do today.  Determination in reaching a goal or accomplishing a task will lead to total success.

---

## November 12

### *"There is only one time that is important - NOW!*
### *It is the most important time because it is*
### *the only time we have any power over."*
Leo Tolstoy

John Maxwell said, "If there is hope in the future, there is power in the present."  Action brings results.  Make every moment count.

## November 13

### *"Opportunity does not knock.*
### *You have to find it."*
Sumner Redstone

Search every possibility in every situation to try and discover another avenue to help reach your goals. Don't hesitate to try something new. Step outside your comfort zone and reach for the stars.

## November 14

### *"Take stands, take risks, take responsibility."*
Muriel Siebert

The old saying, "If it is to be, it is up to me" is so true. You must stand for what you believe and take the risk of swimming upstream against the current. You are the only one who can use your talent and skill. Go do it!

## November 15

*"The uncreative mind can spot wrong answers, but it takes a very creative mind to spot wrong questions."*
Anthony Jay

Ask yourself two questions of everything that happens. 1) What is great about this? This will initiate the positive thinking process. 2) How can I make it better? This will start the creative thinking process which will re-enforce the positive thinking process. Before long you will have changed the way you view everything and everyone.

## November 16

*"Don't worry about people stealing your ideas. If your ideas are any good, you'll have to ram them down people's throats."*
Howard Aiken

Someone said, "Ideas are a dime-a-dozen, but those who put them into practice are priceless." Put your ideas to work and watch people get on board.

## November 17

*"There are only three decisions in life. The three great decisions are: 1) Whom are you going to live your life with? 2) What are you going to live your life in? 3) What are you going to live your life for?"*
Charlie "Tremendous" Jones

Life is really simple. Your relationships and your purpose are the most important factors in living life to its fullest. Therefore, create great relationships and discover your purpose and go for it!

## November 18

*"Imagination is more important than knowledge."*
Albert Einstein

Knowledge doesn't require movement. Imagination will lead you to action. Get a picture of what you want to achieve and where you want to end life. Then start down that path!

## November 19

*"Nothing is so embarrassing as watching someone do something that you said could not be done."*
Sam Ewing

My dad always told me, "Never say never". In every sport and every profession there is always someone willing to give it all to exceed the limitations and achieve the impossible. Let it be you!

## November 20

*If you don't continue to grow you'll be like last night's cornbread - stale and dry."*
Loretta Lynn

To grow means to change. Are you willing to change to do the things others only dream about?

## November 21

*"Most of what we say and do is not essential. If you can eliminate it, you'll have more time, and more tranquility. Ask yourself at every moment, 'Is this necessary?'"*
Marcus Aurelius

Audit yourself and determine what is important and what can be eliminated. You'll find that you will have more time for the truly important things. You'll be more efficient and effective. You will defiantly live happier, healthier and probably far more content.

## November 22

*"If you can't live through adversity, you'll never be good at what you do. You have to live through the unfair things, and you have to develop the hide to not let it bother you and keep your eyes focused on what you have to do.'"*
Maurice "Hank" Greenberg

Focus on the positive not the negative. Keep your goals in mind and learn to brush aside the things that could hinder your success. Remember, no one can do it like you do it!

## November 23

*"Listen with regard when others talk. Give your time and energy to others; let others have their own way; do things for reasons other than furthering your own needs."*
Larry Scherwitz

Remember what Zig Zigler says, "If you help enough other people get what they want you will get what you want." A man named Paul said something similar when he said, "What you do for others, God will do for you." What you do for those around you will determine how far you go in life.

## November 24

*"Success seems to be connected with action. Successful people keep moving. They make mistakes, but they don't quit."*
Conrad Hilton

Those successful folks we study and admire in history seem to always have difficulty. Some failed many times in many ways, but they aren't remembered for their failures only their achievements. Never quit, never give up and never give your attention to negative people. You can do it!

## November 25

*"There is no such thing as a problem without a solution, only problems for which we do not yet have enough information to know what the solution is. When you have enough information, it is easy to solve a problem."*
Jose Silva

You are a problem solver. Realize that all things are possible and every problem can be solved. It may require more research and experimentation, but you can find the answer. The more problems you solve the more opportunities will come your way. Don't hesitate, take action and solve a problem today!

## November 26

*"Few people take objectives really seriously. They put average effort into too many things, rather than superior thought and effort into a few important things. People who achieve the most are selective as well as determined."*
Richard Koch

Prioritize your tasks and give your greatest efforts into those that rank highest. Delegate to others those tasks that can be accomplished easily.

165

## November 27

*"If there is a trait which does characterize leaders it is opportunism. Successful people are very often those who steadfastly refuse to be daunted by disadvantage and have the ability to turn disadvantage to good effect. They are people who seize opportunity and take risks. Leadership then seems to be a matter of personality and character."*
John Viney Drive

Opportunities are more evident to those who are optimistic. Optimistic leaders are always looking and expecting the best. They are focusing on the good not the bad in every person, situation or circumstance. Be that leader!

## November 28

*"The basic difference between people who live their dreams and those who only dream about how they would live, are the accuracy of their plans, their ability to generate new ideas, and their ability to take action."*
Unknown

The old song that says, "If you want to go somewhere, you've got to be somebody" is correct. You must know what you want, why you want it and put a plan in place to get where you want to go. And most importantly you must measure yourself continually to see your progress and if you are not making any, change your approach until you see results.

166

## November 29

*"A good plan implemented today is better than a perfect plan implemented tomorrow."*
George Patton

Just as you have read many times the key to success is action. Getting started is vital. You can change your approach and strategy as you go, but you must execute the plan.

## November 30

*"The biggest disability is a negative attitude."*
Axel Ghien

Most negative people never realize they are disabled. There is no way to number the sales lost, marriages failed, friendships destroyed all because of a poor attitude. You can either have a negative attitude or a positive attitude, the choice is yours. People with positive attitudes are normally happier, have more friends, live longer and attract more business. Be POSITIVE!!!

## December 1

### *"An idea is worthless unless you use it."*
John Maxwell

So many of us have great ideas that are never carried out and when we hear of someone else who had the same idea, but put legs to it we tend to get upset. When you get an idea that will benefit others, act on it and see where it takes you.

## December 2

### *"Success comes to the person who does today what you were thinking about doing tomorrow."*
unknown

If you're thinking of tackling a business idea, creating a product or establishing a relationship, then do not wait. Those who wait for the right time, enough money, or the perfect people will lose. Do it now!

## December 3

***"You may be disappointed if you fail,
But you are doomed if you don't try."***
Beverly Sills

People fail every day. The key to success is getting up and trying again. A study of over 300 world class leaders found that 50% were raised in poverty and 50% of them had a physical disability. But they never let circumstances stand in their way of achieving their goal. You shouldn't either!

## December 4

***"Accept the challenges so that you may feel
the exhilaration of victory."***
General George S. Patton, Jr.

The cliché "There is no gain without pain" is one most of us never like to hear. However, there can be no victory without overcoming obstacles or difficulties. So accept that fact and reach for the stars. You will be surprised what you can achieve.

## December 5

*"There are two primary choices in life:*
*to accept conditions as they exist, or*
*accept the responsibility for changing them."*
Denis Waitley

You have the choice of being like a thermometer or thermostat. You can either gage the things that go on around you or you can make the choice to try and change them. Don't be afraid, make a choice!

## December 6

**"While you, the leader, can teach many things, character is not taught easily to adults who arrive at your desk lacking it. Be cautious about taking on** *reclamation projects* **regardless of the talent they may possess. Have the courage to make character count among the qualities you seek in others."**
John Wooden

I've been told that we all have three characters—the one which we exhibit, the one we really have, and the one which we think we have. Surrounding yourself with people of good character is vital to developing a winning organization.

### December 7

*"God gave us two ends; one to sit on and one to think with. Our success in life will be determined by which one we use the most."*
Unknown

Today is the greatest opportunity you have to be bold, creative, grateful and successful. Don't waste a minute! Use you brains and be the leader, the motivator, the friend, and the success you want to become. When you see it, others will also!

### December 8

*"Regardless of your current position, become the CAO, the Chief Attitude Officer of your organization."*
Donny Ingram

Be consistent in your leadership and set the example every day. Treat everyone as an important individual. Involve your entire team in setting goals and recognize them for great ideas. Provide every person the feeling they're valuable. Be inspirational, uplifting and motivational.

## December 9

*"To lead people, walk beside them ... As for the best leaders, the people do not notice their existence. The next best, the people honor and praise. The next, the people fear; and the next, the people hate ... When the best leader's work is done the people say, 'We did it ourselves!'"*
Lao-tsu

When your team does great, be the leader that says they did it. When things don't go so well, be the leader that says I did it.

## December 10

*"Dictators ride to and fro upon tigers which they dare not dismount. And the tigers are getting hungry."*
Winston Churchill

Most dictators rule with fear, manipulation and intimidation. Sooner or later they will be eaten. Lead with care, compassion and confidence. In doing so you will not only win but leave a legacy that will last forever!

## December 11

*"Enthusiasm is the thing that will make you great,*
*it will pull you out of the mediocre and*
*commonplace and build power into you."*
Author Unknown

Enthusiasm gives you a glow and lights up your face. It is the maker of friends and the producer of confidence. It lets the world know that you've got what it takes. It is the inspiration that will make you "wake up and live." It puts spring in your step and a twinkle in your eyes. It can change a dead salesperson into a phenomenal producer, a pessimist into an optimist. If you have it, you should thank God for it. If you don't have it, then you should get down on your knees and pray to have it for the year ahead.

## December 12

*"Unless we think of others and do something for them, we*
*miss one of the greatest sources of happiness."*
Ray Lyman Wilbur

Physiologists tell us that the greatest way to achieve the feeling we want is by doing something nice for someone else. Plan each day to invest in other people and enjoy the thrill of living your life.

## December 13

### *"The only gift is a portion of thyself."*
Ralph Waldo Emerson

The greatest gift you can give is yourself. Offer your time, resources and talents to help others and you'll be able to live life with joy, peace and love.

---

## December 14

### *"Not being able to do everything is no excuse for not doing everything you can."*
Ashleigh Brilliant"

Don't wait until you have all you think you need before taking action. Use what you have now to do what you can.

## December 15

*"The value of a man resides in what he gives*
*and not in what he is capable of receiving."*
Albert Einstein

This is a life principle. When we can give we set in motion a positive response that we will benefit from in the future. Give of your time, resources and skills to provide assistance for others.

## December 16

*"He who cannot give anything away*
*cannot feel anything either."*
Friedrich Nietzsche

According to medical science when you give it causes the brain to produce chemicals that provide you a good feeling. Therefore, we are in control of how we feel.

## December 17

***"We make a living by what we get,
but we make a life by what we give."***
Winston Churchill

People will not remember you for what you obtain but they will never forget what you give to increase their life. Be a giver!

---

## December 18

***"Think of giving not as a duty, but as a privilege."***
John D. Rockefeller Jr.

Giving is a choice. You have the power to decide to be the change or the miracle for someone in need. Maybe it is only a smile, but give it from the heart.

## December 19

*"Remember that there is no happiness in having or in getting, but only in giving. Reach out. Share. Smile. Hug. Happiness is a perfume you cannot pour on others without getting a few drops on yourself."*
Og Mandino

Every person on this earth wants and needs to know they are wanted, needed and valued. You can provide those you come into contact with that feeling. By doing so, you will spread happiness daily.

## December 20

*"Every time we open our mouths to speak or sing we are affecting ourselves and the people hearing us. By opening up your voice to its greatest possibilities, you will experience positive changes both physically and emotionally. Change the way you sound and enjoy the success it will bring to you."*
Roger Love

You can transform your image, enhance your career, and present your best self simply by improving your speaking voice. Practice how you speak and always use words of encouragement.

## December 21

*"You have not lived today until you have done something for someone who can never repay you."*
John Bunyon

Life is about feelings. You can experience the greatest feelings when you help someone without them knowing it was you. Never pass up an opportunity to use your power to touch the lives of others.

## December 22

*"No person was ever honored for what he received. Honor has been the reward for what he gave."*
Calvin Coolidge
*Former American President*

Metals, trophies, ribbons and plaques are presented to those who gave of themselves, their talents and their skills. Most were rewarded for what they did for others.

## December 23

*"Since you get more joy out of giving joy to others, you should put a good deal of thought into the happiness that you are able to give."*
Eleanor Roosevelt

This is the time of year we buy gifts for those we love. Think about what you can give to those around you to enrich their lives. Remember, it's not the price, it is the thought and effort that brings joy to others.

## December 24

*"My heart aches for the boy whose dad sends him off for an education before teaching him a little of the why and 'After spending a lifetime in management development, I'm convinced that spiritual growth is more important than education; you can get an education and not grow, but you can't help getting an education if you grow spiritually."*
Charlie "Tremendous" Jones

I'm also saddened by parents who refuse to teach the value and power of spiritual beliefs. I'm even more disappointed that people try to lead others with no commitment to their own beliefs. Our values, morals and standards are based on our personal beliefs. Make a decision and stand for something or you will fall for anything.

## December 25

*"Yesterday is history. Tomorrow is a mystery.*
*Today is a gift. That's why it is called the present."*
Alice Morse Earle

The clock is running. Make the most of today. Time waits for no man. What have you done today to show you gratitude.

---

## December 26

*"Never, for the sake of peace and quiet,*
*deny your own experience or convictions."*
Dag Hammarskjold

In today's world sometimes we are asked to put our convictions aside to appease someone else. When we do we lose a little more of self. Never waiver and never give in on what you believe.

## December 27

*"In the long run, we shape our lives, and we shape ourselves. The process never ends until we die. And the choices we make are ultimately our own responsibility.*
Eleanor Roosevelt

We are the only creatures born on this planet with the ability to choose. All the other creatures are born with what we call instinct. They do things they can't even question like bears hibernating, geese flying south, salmon swimming upstream. But you and I as human creatures are given a choice. We choose everyday actions and ideas that will shape and form our future. What choices will you make this coming year?

## December 28

*"All blame is a waste of time. No matter how much fault you find with another, and regardless of how much you blame him, it will not change you."*
Wayne Dyer

Step outside the blame-game and take responsibility. It doesn't matter who caused it, when you take responsibility you become the better person and you receive the benefits.

## December 29

*"What we have done for ourselves alone dies with us;*
*what we have done for others and the world remains*
*and is immortal."*
Albert Pike

Do you want to live, love, laugh and leave a legacy or complain, blame, hate and leave lunacy? The choice is yours!

## December 30

*"If a man does not know to what port he is steering, no*
*wind is favorable to him."*
Seneca

The time is now to plan, not just what you want to accomplish next year, but where you want to end up in this life. Make the time to plan, prepare and then expect to achieve your goals.

## December 31

*"Decide upon your major definite purpose in life and
then organize all your activities around it."*
Brian Tracy

One of the greatest needs today is for people to discover
their true purpose in life.  What are you here to do?  It
centers on your gifts, talents and abilities.  You are
designed for a specific purpose.  Once you discover your
purpose you are on your way to a life of contentment and
significance.

## AUTHOR

I truly hope the quotes and thoughts in this book are helpful in keeping you moving forward. The world we live and work in today is full of negative and de-motivating material. We must discipline our minds to focus on the positive and keep our eyes on the goal if we are to experience the success we were meant to achieve.

*Donny Ingram*

For more information about the author, other books or to order additional copies of this book please visit:
www.donnyingram.com

## OTHER BOOKS

## *Winning the BATTLE*

All through life we face situations and circumstances and it seems we have to battle every step of the way to overcome most of them. This book is about the principles that will give you the edge in taking personal responsibility in winning the battle. It is written with wit, humor and wisdom to help equip every reader in reaching their full potential in life. As you will see these principles are being use by thousands of successful people today. Donny uses humor, wisdom and personal experiences to show how effective these principles are when put into practice. This book is an easy and fun read and a must for anyone seeking an avenue to success and significance.

To purchase the book visit:
www.ingrammanagement.com/positiveprintmedia

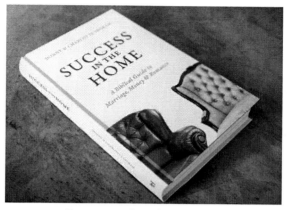

## *Success in the Home*

Success in the Home is a Biblical guide for Marriage, Money and Romance. It is an outstanding guidebook for the marriage relationship. Everyone desiring to learn the principles that will bring love, joy, trust, respect and dedication should read this book. It is a roadmap for singles looking to get married, newly weds just getting started or those who have been married for many years. It is a valuable resource for every home desiring a marriage that will produce health, wealth and happiness. It's also a wonderful gift to help show others the way to achieve success in the home.

To purchase the book visit:
www.ingrammanagement.com/positiveprintmedia

## *Train My Hands to War*

Donny & Charlotte Ingram have written this book to help each Christian understand how to follow God's Word when it comes to achieving success with finances. In today's troubled economic times we can have peace, confidence and security. David said, *"Train my hands to war and my fingers to do battle."* There are three ways to war against the enemy with your hands; Pray, Praise and Give. In this new book Donny & Charlotte outline God's principles for giving. They examine each principle and what the promises are for each. You'll find scripture references for each principle and how to use money as a weapon to destroy the bondage of debt and oppression and really understand how to have peace over your finances.

To purchase the book visit:
www.ingrammanagement.com/positiveprintmedia

## *M&M Leadership*
### *(Mentoring or Manipulating)*

This is a book everyone should read. We all are looking to someone or we have someone looking to us for guidance and direction. Many feel that situations and circumstances in life are overwhelming and they need help to navigate through the tough stuff in order to succeed and reach their full potential. The problem is, some leaders use manipulation to control people instead of leading them; others use manipulation to gain power instead of instilling purpose; and many use manipulation to reach personal goals rather than building people to fulfill their own destiny. M&M leadership is a guide to help those who are looking to develop the world's most valuable asset – People.

To purchase the book visit:
www.ingrammanagement.com/positiveprintmedia